NINE LECTURES

ON

BEES

Given in 1923 to the Workmen at the Goetheanum

BY

Rudolf Steiner, Ph.D.

PRINTED AS MANUSCRIPT, FROM A SHORTHAND REPORT UNREVISED BY THE LECTURER, BY KIND PERMISSION OF FRAU MARIE STEINER. ALL RIGHTS RESERVED. TRANSLATIONS, COPYING, ETC. STRICTLY FORBIDDEN.

Copy No. 378

Edited for The Natural Science Section of the Goetheanum, Dornach

BY

DR. G. WACHSMUTH

ANTHROPOSOPHICAL AGRICULTURAL FOUNDATION

1933.

This is an exact copy of the original publication, Dornach 1929

Nine Lectures on Bees by Rudolf Steiner, Ph.D.
© 2020 Published by Northern Bee Books

All rights reserved. No part of this publication may be reproduced, stored in a retrieval system, transmitted in any form or by any means electronic, mechanical, including photocopying, recording or otherwise without prior consent of the copyright holders.

ISBN 978-1-912271-63-4

Northern Bee Books is a trading name for Peacock Press Ltd
Scout Bottom Farm
Mytholmyoyd
Hebden Bridge
HX7 5JS (UK)
www.northernbeebooks.co.uk

Top cover photograph © John Phipps

Design and artwork
DM Design and Print

NINE LECTURES

ON

BEES

GIVEN IN 1923 TO THE WORKMEN AT THE GOETHEANUM

BY

Rudolf Steiner, Ph.D.

Editor's Preface

THE following lectures were given by Rudolf Steiner to the workmen employed on the building of the Goetheanum. For some years Rudolf Steiner had almost every week devoted an hour to the spiritual welfare of those who laboured, whether as masons, smiths, plasterers or joiners, etc., in the erection of the building he had planned. They were an expression of the gratitude of his so kindly-human, social nature to those who co-operated with him in the completion of this remarkable building.

Usually, the work-people would assemble in the temporary lecture room in the Schreinerei, and Rudolf Steiner would ask them for questions, to which he would give immediate impromptu replies out of the inexhaustible well-spring of his spiritual and practical knowledge.

Thus arose these lectures on the nature of bees, wasps and ants, for among the workers were many bee-keepers who asked him questions on these subjects.

The lectures were therefore, neither previously prepared nor were they assigned to any special theme. They were not given to a gathering of professional, expert bee-keepers, nor to any specialist circle, but arose out of the quite unexpected questions and answers, sayings and gainsayings between Rudolf Steiner and the workmen.

This background, as also the content of the lectures and the way in which they were delivered, must be kept in view, for they were naturally not concerned with detailed instructions on bee-keeping, but rather with giving his listeners some understanding of the spiritual relationships in Nature, and especially in connection with the nature of the bees.

During these years Rudolf Steiner was thus able to give the work people a comprehensive world-picture, and we others who at that time were not permitted to share the lectures specially devoted to them, have often envied the workers these beautiful hours.

All who are interested in bees will find in them not only a rich and suggestive content, but also a deep understanding of the Spiritual in Nature.

FOR THE NATURAL SCIENCE SECTION
AT THE GOETHEANUM
DR. GUENTHER WACHSMUTH

Dornach, 1929.

LECTURE I.

Dornach, February 3, 1923.

GOOD morning, gentlemen! Since our last meeting have you thought of any question you would like to ask me?

(A question was asked as to the effects of absinthe, also a question as to the difference between bees and wasps.)

Dr. Steiner:

In asking his question the gentleman in the audience, as an expert bee-master, draws attention to the differences between the life of the bees and that of the wasps. There is much that is similar here, and I have recently described the life of the wasps to you. The life of the bees much resembles it, but, on the other hand, in the bee-hive there is a very special and remarkable life. How can we account for this?

You see, this cannot be fully explained without the faculty of spiritual perception. That the life of the hive is extraordinarily wisely organised no one who has ever observed it can deny. Naturally, no one can say that the bees have the same kind of intelligence that men have, for we certainly have the instrument of the brain, whereas the bees have nothing of the kind; thus the universal world wisdom cannot be drawn into their bodies in the same way. But influences coming from the whole surrounding universe do, none the less, work with immense power in the bee-hive. Indeed, one can only arrive at a right understanding of what the life of the bees truly is, when one takes into account that the whole environment of the earth has a very great influence upon the life of the colony. This life within the hive rests upon the fact that the bees, to a much greater extent than the ants and wasps, work so completely together, so arranging their whole activity that everything is in harmony.

If one would understand how this comes about, one must say: In the life of the bee everything that in other creatures expresses itself as sexual life is, in the case of the bees, suppressed, very remarkably suppressed; it is very much driven into the background. For you see, in the case of the bees, reproduction is limited to quite a few exceptional female individuals—the Queen bees—to a very few chosen individuals, for in the others the sexual life is more or less suppressed.

But it is *love* that is present in the life of sex, and love belongs to the realm of the soul; and further, through the fact that certain organs of the body are worked upon by forces of the soul, these organs become able to reveal, to express love. Thus, because all this is driven into the background in the nature of the bees, and reserved for the Queen bee alone, the whole otherwise sexual life of the colony is transformed into those activities which the bees develop among themselves.

It was for this reason that in olden times, wise men who had a knowledge of all this quite different from the knowledge of men today, that these wise men related the whole wonderful activity within the hive to the life of love, to that part of life which they connected with the planet Venus.

If we describe the wasps and ants we can say they are creatures which, in a certain sense, withdraw from the influence of Venus, whereas the bees surrender themselves entirely to Venus, unfolding a life of love throughout the whole hive. This life will be filled with wisdom; you can well imagine how wise it must be!

I have already told you various things about the reproductive process and the unconscious wisdom contained in it. This unconscious wisdom is unfolded by the bees in their external activity. What we only experience when love arises in our hearts is to be found, as it were, in the whole bee-hive as substance. The whole hive is in reality permeated with love. The individual bees renounce love in manifold ways, and thus develop love throughout the whole hive. One only begins to understand the life of the bees when one knows that the bee lives in an atmosphere completely pervaded by love.

On the other hand the bee is quite especially favoured by the fact that, in its turn, it feeds upon just those parts of the plants which are also wholly pervaded by love. The bees suck out their food—which they then turn into honey—exclusively from those parts of the plants that are centred in love; they bring, so to speak, the love-life of the flowers into the hive.

Hence one must say that the life of the bees must be studied by making use of the soul.

This is much less necessary when we study the ants and the wasps for we shall see that here, though they withdraw themselves to some extent, still they do surrender themselves more to sexual life. With the exception of the Queen, the bees are actually beings which, as I would like to put it, say to themselves " We will renounce the individual sexual life that we make ourselves ' bearers of love.' " Thus they have been able to bring what lives in the flowers into the hive; and when you begin really to think this out rightly, you will reach the whole mystery of the bee-hive.

The life of this sprouting, budding love which is in the flowers is there too, within the honey. You can also study what honey does, when you eat it yourself. What does the honey do? When honey is eaten it furthers the right connection in man between the airy and the watery elements. Nothing is better for man than to add the right proportion of honey to his food. For in a wonderful way the bees see to it that man learns to work with his soul upon the organs of his body. In the honey the bee gives back again to man what he needs to further the activity of his soul-forces within his body. Thus when man adds some honey to his food, he wishes so to prepare his soul that it may work rightly within his body—breathe rightly.

Bee-keeping is therefore something that greatly helps to advance our civilisation, for it makes men strong.

You see, when one realises that the bees receive very many influences from the starry worlds, one sees also how they can pass on to man what is fitted for him. All that is living, when it is rightly combined, works rightly together. When one stands before a hive of bees one should say quite solemnly to oneself: " By way of the bee-hive the whole Cosmos enters man and makes him strong and able."

LECTURE II.

Dornach, November 26, 1923.

[In connection with a paper read to the work-people by Herr Müller]

GOOD morning, gentlemen! I will add just a few remarks to the statements made by Herr Müller—remarks which may perhaps be of interest to you, though naturally, as far as the present day is concerned, the time has not yet come when one could really apply these things in practical bee-keeping. For the moment, on this side of practical bee-keeping, very little, or perhaps not even anything much can be said, since Herr Müller has already given you a beautiful account of the way things are managed nowadays.

If you listened to him attentively it must have occurred to you that this whole question of bee-keeping has something of the nature of a riddle. Obviously, the bee-keeper is first of all interested in what he has to do. Everyone must, in reality, take the greatest interest in bee-keeping, for in fact, more in human life depends on it than one usually thinks.

Let us look at it in a wider sense. As you have heard in the lectures Herr Müller has given you here, the bees are able to gather what is already present as nectar in the plants. They really only gather the nectar, and then we men take away as honey a portion of what was collected for the hive—on the whole it is not a very large portion. We might say that what man takes away is somewhere about 20%—roughly speaking.

But in addition to this the bee, by means of its bodily structure and organisation, can also take pollen from the plants. Thus the bee gathers from the plant something that exists there in very minute quantities and is difficult to procure. Pollen is collected by the bees, with the help of the minute brushes attached to their bodies, in the very, very small quantities in which, relatively speaking, it is available; this pollen is then stored away, or consumed in the hive.

In the bee we therefore have a creature before us that collects a substance extremely delicately prepared by Nature, and having done so, makes use of it in its own household.

Now we will go a step further, to something very seldom noticed because one does not stop to think about it. Having transformed the food by means of its own bodily substances into wax—this the bee produces out of itself—the bee now makes a special little container in which to deposit its eggs, or in which to store up food supplies. This special little vessel is, I should like to say, a really great marvel. It appears to be hexagonal when we look at it from above; looked at from the side it is closed in this way. (Diagrams 1 and 2.) Eggs can be deposited there, or food can be stored. Each vessel lies next to another; they fit extremely well together, so that this "surface" by which one cell, (for so it is called), is joined to another in the honey-comb, is exceedingly well made use of—the space is well used.

When the question is raised how can the bee instinctively build so skilfully formed a cell, people generally answer: "It is done that the space may be thoroughly well used." That is true. If you try to imagine any other form of cell there would always be spaces, everything is joined together so that every part of the surface of the comb is completely made use of.

This certainly is one reason, but you see it is not the only reason. We must consider how the little larva which lies within it is entirely isolated, and one must not by any means believe that anything exists in Nature that is without forces. This six-angled, six-surfaced dwelling has certain forces within it; it would be quite another matter if the larva were to occupy a round one. In Nature it signifies something quite definite that it lies within this six-surfaced little dwelling-place. The larva receives the forces of the *form*; later it feels in its body that it was once in this hexagonally-formed cell, in its youth when it was quite soft.

The bee is afterwards able to build similar cells out of the same forces which it thus absorbed. There lie the forces through which the bee afterwards works, for what the bee *makes* externally lies in its environment.

This is the first thing we must notice. Now there is another very remarkable fact that has been described to you. In the hive there is a variety of cells. I think every bee-keeper can well distinguish between the cells of the worker-bees and those of the drones. This is not a difficult matter, is it? It is still easier to distinguish between the cells of worker-bees and drones and those of the Queens, for the latter have not at all this form, they are more like a sack. The Queen cells have no such shape, they are more like a kind of sack; also there are very few of them in the hive. So we must say: The worker-bees and the drones (the males) develop in hexagonal cells, but the Queen is developed in a "sack." She is not at all concerned to have hexagonal surroundings. (Diagram 3 and 4).

Then we must consider something else. You see, the Queen for her development, *i.e.* until she is a complete full-grown insect, needs only sixteen days. She is then fully matured. A worker bee requires about twenty-one days to mature, which is a longer period. One might say that Nature bestows much more care on the development of the worker-bee than on that of the Queen.

But we shall soon see that quite another reason comes in question. The worker-bee then, needs twenty-one days, and the drone, the male—which will finish its task soonest of all—needs twenty-three to twenty-four days. The males are killed when they have fulfilled their task.

We have quite a new situation here. The different kinds of bees—Queens, workers and drones—all need a different number of days for their development.

Well, let us consider these twenty-one days needed by the worker-bees. There is something very special about this. A period of twenty-one days is not without meaning for what happens on the earth. Twenty-one days are equal to the period of time during which the Sun, approximately speaking, revolves once upon its own axis.

Now think, the worker-bee takes just that period of time for its development which the Sun takes to turn upon its axis. The worker-bee experiences one revolution of the Sun, and because it has experienced one complete revolution it enters into all the Sun can give.

If it wished to go further it would always meet only with the same Sun-influences, for if you picture to yourselves here the worker-bee, *(Diagram 5) and here the Sun at the moment when the egg is laid, then here we shall have the point exactly opposite the Sun. The Sun revolves upon its own axis once in twenty-one days; then it returns again and the first point is again here. If this were to continue, only such Sun-workings would be there as had once been there already. So the worker-bee by the time it is fully developed has experienced all that the Sun can give. Should the worker-bee continue to develop it must leave the Sun and enter the earth development; it will then no longer be having a Sun-influence in its development because it already had this, and has tasted it to the full. Now it passes into the earth development, but only as a perfect insect, as a matured creature. I might say—the worker-bee occupies herself only momentarily with this earth-development, and has then finished with her Sun-development, is entirely a creature of the Sun.

Now let us look at the drone. The drone, I might say, considers the matter a little longer. It does not think itself quite ready after twenty-one days, so before it is fully matured it enters the earth-development. The drone is thus an earthly being, whereas the worker-bee is entirely a child of the Sun.

How is it with the Queen? The Queen-bee does not even go through the whole of the Sun-revolution, but stays behind and remains always a creature of the Sun. For this reason the Queen is much nearer to her larval state than the others; the drones (the males) are the farthest removed from the larval state. The Queen is thereby able to lay eggs. In the bees it is clearly to be seen what it signifies to be exposed to the earth-influence or to the Sun-influence. As you know, it depends entirely on whether the bee completes, or does not complete its Sun-development, that it becomes either a Queen, a worker or a drone. The Queen lays eggs, and it is because she remains always under the influence of the Sun and receives nothing from the earth that she is enabled to do so. The worker-bee goes a little further and develops for

---

*Dr. Steiner draws on the blackboard.

another four or five days; it tastes the Sun to the full. But then, just when its body becomes firm enough it goes over, just for a moment, as I said, into the earth-development. Thus the worker-bee cannot return again to the Sun, for it has already thoroughly absorbed its influences. Consequently the worker-bee cannot lay eggs.

The drones are the males; they can fertilise; this power of fertilisation comes from the earth; the drones acquire it in the few days during which they continue their growth within the earth-evolution and before they reach maturity. So we can now say: in the bees it is clearly to be seen that fertilisation (male fecundation) comes from the earthly forces, and the female capacity to develop the egg comes from the forces of the Sun. So you see, you can easily imagine how significant is the length of time during which a creature develops. This is very important for, naturally, something happens within a definite time which could not occur in either a shorter or a longer time, for then quite other things would happen.

But there is something further to be considered. You see, the Queen develops in sixteen days. Then the point which stood opposite to her in the Sun is perhaps only *here*; *(Diagram 5) the Queen remains within the Sun-development. The remaining part of the Sun's course is gone through by the worker-bees, but they too remain within the Sun-development; they do not really pass out of it to the earth. And so, you see, they feel themselves entirely akin to the Queen because they belong to the same Sun-influence; the whole host of the worker-bees feel themselves related to the Queen. They say:—"The drones are betrayers; they have fallen to the earth. They no longer belong to us; we suffer them only because we need them."

For what are they needed?

As you know, it sometimes happens that the Queen is not fertilised; nevertheless she lays eggs. The Queen need not necessarily be fertilised to lay eggs. Then we have what is called "virgin-brood." This also happens with other insects; the scientific name for it is parthenogenesis. But only drones can emerge from these unfertilised eggs; no workers and no Queens. Thus when a Queen is unfertilised, worker-bees and Queens do not hatch out, only drones; such a colony is naturally useless.

You see, in "virgin-brood" only the *opposite* sex is produced, not the *same* sex. This is a very interesting fact, and an important one in the whole household of Nature—namely, that fertilisation is necessary if the same sex is to come into being (this applies to the lower animals of course, not to the higher ones). With the bees it is the case that only drones emerge where fertilisation has not taken place.

This fecundation of the bee is indeed a very special affair; there is nothing like a marriage-bed to which one retires, it all takes an entirely different course. It takes place openly, in the

---

*Drawing on the blackboard.

full sun-light and, though this may seem very strange at first, as high as possible in the air. The Queen-bee flies as far as possible towards the Sun to which she belongs. (I have already described this to you), and that drone alone which can overcome the earthly forces—for the drones have united themselves with the earthly forces—only that drone which can fly the highest is able to fecundate the Queen up there in the air.

The Queen returns and lays her eggs. So you see, the bees have no marriage-bed, they have a marriage flight; they must strive as far as they are able, towards the Sun. One must have, is it not so, fine weather for this marriage flight which really needs the Sun? In bad weather it cannot take place.

Now all this shows you how closely the Queen remains related to the Sun. When fertilisation has taken place, then worker-bees emerge from the worker-cells; first the little larvæ appear, as Herr Müller has so well described, and then after twenty-one days develop into worker-bees. In the sack-like cells a Queen develops.

Now if we are to go further, I must tell you something you may naturally receive with some doubt, for it needs exact study. Nevertheless, it really is so. I will link this further matter to the following:—The worker-bee now mature and ready, sets out on its flight, visiting the flowers and trees to which it attaches itself by the minute hooks on its feet. (Diagram 6) It gathers both nectar and pollen. The pollen is carried on the body where there is a special contrivance for depositing it; the nectar it sucks up with its tongue. A part of the nectar is used for its own food, but the greater part is retained and this, on its return to the hive, the bee spits out. Actually, when we eat honey we eat the spittle of the bee; we must be quite clear as to this, but it is a very clean and sweet spittle.

Thus the bee gathers all it needs for food, for storing, and for further elaboration into wax, etc. Now we must ask ourselves, how does the bee find its way to the flowers? It finds its way to the flowers with absolute certainty, but one is quite unable to explain this by merely observing the eyes of the bee. The worker-bee (the drone has somewhat larger eyes), has only two small eyes, one at each side, and three quite minute ones on the forehead (Diagram 7). The drones have rather larger eyes. But when one studies these two eyes of the bee, one discovers that it sees very little with them, and that with the three minute frontal eyes it sees, to begin with, nothing at all. That is the strange thing—that the bee does not find the flowers by sight, but by a sense more like the sense of smell. It finds its way to the flowers by a sense which is between taste and smell, on its flight it already, as it were, *tastes* the pollen and the nectar. From far away it tastes them, so the bee has no need to use its eyes at all.

Now make for yourself a clear picture of the following.

Think of a Queen-bee born in the realm of the Sun, and not having tasted the Sun's working to the full, has remained, so to speak, entirely under the influence of the Sun. The whole host of the worker-bees, though it has completed the course of the Sun's revolution, has not actually passed over to the earth development. These worker-bees feel themselves united with the Queen, not because they were under the *same* Sun, but because they remained within the Sun-development; this is why they feel themselves so united with the Queen. In their development they did not sever themselves from that of the Queen. The drones do not belong to them; they have separated themselves.

But now the following happens. In order that a new Queen can come into being, the marriage flight must have taken place. The Queen goes out into the Sun. A new Queen comes into being. At that moment a most remarkable thing happens to the whole host of the workers who feel themselves so united with the old Queen. Their tiny little eyes *begin to see* when the new Queen is born. This they cannot endure; they cannot endure that that which they themselves are, should come from elsewhere. The three minute frontal eyes, these three very small eyes of the worker-bees, are built up from within; they are permeated with the inner blood and so on, of the bee; they were never exposed to the external working of the Sun. But now the new Queen is born from out of the Sun, and brings Sun-light with her own body into the hive; now the bees become—I should like to say—clairvoyant with their little eyes. They cannot endure this light of the new Queen. The whole host of them prepares to swarm. It is like fear of the new Queen, as though they were dazzled. It is as though we were to look at the Sun itself.

That is why the bees swarm. And now one has once more to re-establish the colony on the basis of the majority of the worker-bees which still belong to the hive—that is, to the old Queen. The new Queen must find a new people. A part of the population of the hive has of course, remained behind, but these are those born under different circumstances. The reason why the bees swarm lies in the fact that the workers cannot endure the new Queen who brings in a new Sun-influence.

Now you might ask, "Why should the bees feel so sensitive towards this new Sun-influence?" This is indeed a very strange thing. No doubt you know that it is sometimes not at all pleasant to meet a bee; it may sting one. If one is so large an animal as man at the worst one gets an inflamed skin; all the same it is rather unpleasant. Smaller animals may even die from the sting of a bee. This is due to the fact that the sting is really a tube in which a kind of piston moves up and down, which is connected with a poison bag. This poison (very disagreeable to one who has to experience it) is however, of great value to the bees. It is by no means pleasant for the bee to have to part with its poison, and in reality it only does so because it cannot bear that any influence from outside should approach. The bee wants always to remain within itself, to stay within the sphere of its own substance. Every external influence is felt as disturbing, as something to be warded off by its poison. But this poison has at the same time quite another significance, for in the minutest quantities it continually passes over into the whole body of the bee; without it the bee could not exist at all.

One must understand in studying the worker-bee that it is unable to see with its small frontal eyes, and that this is due to the fact that the poison continually permeates these frontal eyes. The moment the new Queen appears with her new Sun-influence, this poison is harmfully affected. It ceases to be active, and the small eyes suddenly begin to see, for the fact that the bee lives its life in a perpetual twilight is due to the poison.

If I were to describe to you in a pictorial form what the bee experiences when a new Queen slips out of her sack-like cell, I should have to say: "The bee lives always in the twilight, and finds its way about by means of a sense between taste and smell; it lives in a twilight congenial to it. But when the new Queen appears it is exactly like when we walk in the twilight of a June evening, and the little glow-worms are shining." Even so does the new Queen shine for the swarm, because the poison does not work strongly enough to keep the bees in their twilight seclusion from the world. It keeps within it even when it flies out, because it is then able with its poison to keep within itself. It needs the poison when it fears something from outside may disturb it. The whole colony desires to be entirely within itself.

Indeed, in order that the Queen may remain in the sphere of the Sun she may not dwell in an angular cell, but within a circular one. There she remains within the Sun-influence.

Here we touch upon something that makes bee-keeping so extremely interesting for everyone. For you see, in reality, things go on in the hive in exactly the same way as in the human head, only with a slight difference. In our head, for instance, the substances do not grow to such dimensions. In the human head we have nerves, blood-vessels, and the separately situated round-shaped cells which are always to be found. We have these three varieties of cells in the human head. The nerves consist of separate cells which only do not grow into independent beings because Nature encloses them on all sides; in reality, however, these nerves would like to become little animals. If the *nerve-cells* of the human head could develop in all directions, under the same conditions as those of the hive, then the *nerve-cells* would become drones.

The *blood-cells* which flow in the veins would become *worker-bees*; and the *single free cells* which are, above all, in the centre of the head and go through the shortest period of development, may be compared with the *Queen bees*.

So in the human head we have the same three forces (Diagram 8) as in the hive.

Now the workers bring home what they gather from the plants, and work it up in their own bodies into wax, of which they then build the wonderful structure of the combs. The blood-cells of the human head however, do the same thing. From the head they pass into the whole body. When you look for instance, at a bone, at a piece of bone, you will find hexagonal cells everywhere. The blood that circulates through the whole body carries out the same work that is done in the hive by the bees. It is similar with the cells of our muscles which, once more, correspond to the wax-cells of the bees, but these cells being softer, dissolve more quickly, so it is here less noticeable. A study of the bones shows it very well. Thus, the blood has the same forces as those of the worker-bee.

One can even follow their development through the course of time. The cells which you find first developed in the human embryo, and which subsequently remain unchanged, are those that already exist in the early stages of embryonic life. The others, the blood-cells, come into existance somewhat later, and finally the nerve-cells are developed—just as with the beehive. Only man builds up a body which obviously belongs to him; the bee also builds up a body, but for the worker-bees, this body is the honey-comb—the cells. This building of the comb corresponds to what happens within our bodies,—namely, that the blood-cells in reality do this out of a kind of wax—but here it is not so easy to prove.

We ourselves are made of a kind of wax, just as the honey-comb forms the marvellous structure we find in the skep or hive.

So this is how it is. Man has a head, and this head works upon his great body which is actually a "bee-hive" and contains in its relationship between the albuminous cells (which remain round) and the blood, the same connection that exists in the bee-hive between the Queen and the worker-bees. Our nerves are continually destroyed; we continually use up our nervous system. We do not immediately kill our nerves—as the bees kill the drones—for in this case we should die every year, but, none the less, our nerves get weaker every year, and it is through this gradual weakening of the nerves, that man really dies. We are then no longer able to experience our body rightly; a man is actually always dying from the wearing out of his nerves.

When you look at the head—which represents the hive—you find that here all is well protected. If one injures one's head, it is a serious matter; the head cannot bear it. Equally, what happens through the presence of the new Queen—who is there by reason of the marriage flight—is something the bees cannot endure; they prefer to go away rather than remain with her.

This is why bee-keeping has always been regarded as profoundly significant. Man takes away from the bees—perhaps 20% of their honey— and one can justly say that this honey is extremely valuable to man, for with his ordinary food he gets very little honey because honey is distributed in such very small quantities in the plant-world. We get only minute quantities of honey into our bodies in this way.

We also have "bees" within us, namely, our blood, which carries the honey to the various parts of our body. It is honey that the bee needs for producing wax, out of which it then makes the "body" of the colony.

As we grow older, honey has an extremely favourable effect upon us. With children, it is milk that has a similar effect; honey helps us to build our bodies and is thus strongly to be recommended for people who are growing old. It is an exceedingly wholesome food; only one must not eat too much of it! If one eats too much of it, using it not merely as a condiment, one can make the formative forces too strongly active. The form may then get too rigid, and one may develop all kinds of illnesses. A healthy man feels just how much honey he should take. Honey is particularly good for older people because it gives the body the right firmness.

One should also adopt the plan of giving just the right quantity of honey to children suffering from rickets when they are nine to ten months of age, and continue this honey diet till the age of three or four years. Rickets would then not be as bad as it is, for this illness consists in the body being too soft, and collapsing. Of course, in the very first weeks children ought only to be given milk; honey would at that age have no affect. Honey contains the forces that give man's body firmness, These things should be understood.

So one can say that much more attention should be given to the keeping of bees than is usual.

The following is also possible. In Nature everything is wonderfully inter-related. In Nature the laws which man is unable to penetrate with his ordinary intelligence are the most important These laws work—do they not?—always with a perfect freedom. This holds good for instance, with the proportion of the sexes on earth. This is not always the same, the number of men and women is not always, but only more or less an equal one; it is approximately equal over the whole earth. This is brought about in the wisdom of Nature. If it should ever come about—I believe I have already told you this—that men were ultimately able to determine the whole matter arbitrarily, then everything would fall into confusion. If in any country the population has been decimated by wars it will afterwards become more numerous. In Nature, every need calls forth the working of opposite forces.

Now, when the bees seek nectar from the plants, they naturally take this from plants which have also other uses—which give us fruits and so on. But the remarkable thing is that fruit-trees thrive much better in places where bees are kept, than in places where there are no bees.

When the bees take the nectar from the plants Nature does not remain idle, but produces more fruitful plants. So man not only benefits by the honey the bees make, but receives more from the plants visited by the bees. This is a law of great importance, and one we can well understand.

Observing things in this way, one is able to say—in the whole inter-relationship of the bee-colony—of this organism—Nature reveals something very wonderful to us. The bees are subject to forces of Nature which are truly wonderful and of great significance. One cannot but feel shy of fumbling among these forces of Nature. It is becoming increasingly obvious today that wherever man clumsily interferes with these forces he makes matters not better, but worse. He does not make them worse all at once, for it is really so that Nature is everywhere hindered, though notwithstanding these hindrances Nature works as best she may. Certain of these hindrances man can remove, and by doing away with them can make things easier for Nature. For example, he seems actually to be helping Nature when he makes use of beehives which are conveniently arranged, instead of using the old straw skeps.

But here we come to the whole question of artificial bee-keeping. You must not think that I am unable to see—even from a non-anthroposophical point of view—that modern bee-keeping methods seem at first very attractive, for certainly, it makes many things much easier. But the strong holding together—I should like to say—of *one* bee-generation, of one bee-family, will be impaired in the long run.

Speaking generally today, one cannot but praise modern bee-keeping; so long as we see all such precautions observed of which Herr Müller has told us, we must admire them in a certain sense. But we must wait and see how things will be in fifty to eighty years time, for by then certain forces which have hitherto been *organic* in the hive will be mechanised, will become mechanical. It is not possible to bring about that intimate relationship between the colony and a Queen that has been brought, which results naturally when a Queen comes into being in the natural way. Only, at first these things are not observed.

Of course, I by no means wish that a fanatical campaign in opposition to modern bee-keeping should be started, for one cannot do such things in practical life. To do so would be rather like something I will now tell you. It is possible to calculate approximately the time when there will be no more coal in the earth. The coal supply of the earth is exhaustible; one day it will come to an end. Now it would be quite possible to limit the amount of coal taken out of the earth, so that the supply would last as long as the earth itself. One cannot say that we ought to do so, for we should have a little faith for the future. One says " Well, of course we rob the earth of its coal, that is we rob our descendants of coal, but they will be able to invent something else so that they will not need coal any longer." Naturally, one can say the same about the disadvantages of modern bee-keeping !

Still, it is well to be aware of the fact that by working mechanically we destroy what Nature has elaborated in so wonderful a way. You see bee-keeping has at all times been highly valued; in olden times especially, the bee was held to be a sacred animal. Why ? It was so considered because in their whole activity, processes reveal themselves which also take place in man himself. If you take a piece of bees-wax in your hand you are in reality holding something between blood, muscle and bone, which in man's inner organisation passes through the stage of being wax. The wax does not however become solid, but remains fluidic till it is transformed into blood, or muscles, or into the cells of the bones. In the wax we have before us what we bear within us as forces, not as substance.

When men in olden times made candles of the bees-wax and lighted them, they knew that they performed a wonderful and sacred action: "This wax which we now burn we took from the hive; there it was hardened. When the fire melts it and it evaporates, then the wax passes into the same condition in which it is within our own bodies."

In the melting wax of the candle men once apprehended something that rises up to the heavens, something that was also within their own bodies. This awoke a devotional mood in them, and this mood in its turn led them to look upon a bee as a specially sacred creature, because it prepares something which man must continually work out within himself. For this reason, the further back we go the more we find how men approached the bees with reverence. Of course, this was when they were still in their wild state; men found it so, and they looked upon these things as a revelation. Later they brought the bees into their household.

Quite wonderful riddles lie concealed in all that happens with the bees, and by much studying of them one can learn to know what happens between the head and the body in man.

I have now told you a few of those things I wished to speak of. On Wednesday we shall have our next meeting, and perhaps many questions will have arisen. Something may occur also to Herr Müller.

Today I only wished to make these remarks which, after all, are beyond doubt, for they are founded on real knowledge. But, there may still be much that can be made clearer.

LECTURE III.
Dornach, November 28, 1923.

GOOD morning, gentlemen!
Has anything occurred to you that you would like to ask me? (An article was read from the "*Schweizerische Bienenzeitung*" of February-March 1923 entitled "Do Bees perceive colours invisible to Man?")

DR. STEINER.

I will say a few words on this subject. You see, these experiments made by Forel and Kühn show so plainly how thoughtlessly experiments are carried out today. One can naturally not imagine anything more absurd than such an interpretation of these experiments as is given here. Think for a moment that I might do as follows: I might take a substance—there are such substances—specially sensitive to ultra-violet rays, *i.e.*, to colours lying beyond the blue and violet; for instance I take barium platino-cyanide. I exclude all the other colours, let us say, I exclude red, orange, yellow, green, blue—then the indigo would come in and the violet—these also I exclude (Diagram missing.) Now I make a screen; I shut these off in the spectrum; then I have here the so-called ultra-violet rays which are invisible to man. If I now add this substance, this barium platino-cyanide (which is a white powder) then it begins to shine, In a darkened room we see nothing; now we let in these rays, screening them as they come in, allowing therefore, only the ultra-violet rays to enter, which become visible when I introduce barium platino-cyanide. Then one sees it. Then it lights up. Thus, according to this article, I must state that barium platino-cyanide is able to see with some kind of eyes because it shows an activity. But very much the same thing happens if one experiments with ants. Suppose that instead of barium platino-cyanide I take ants; then I exclude the light. The ants run towards the sugar; in the same way barium platino-cyanide lights up. I then say (according to this article) that the ants *see* the ultra-violet rays. But they need to see them just as little as the barium platino-cyanide needs to see in order to shine. All one can really say is, that given a certain substance it produces an effect on the ants. More than that one cannot assert. The scientists concerned are as thoughtless as it is possible to be and make statements that are pure phantasy.

The only thing one can say is this,—that through the sense-organs (once more, according to this article this is proved by the fact that no effect is produced if the eyes of the ants are varnished) that through the sense-organs an impression was made on these insects. It is characteristic that the scientist applies to ants and wasps what he has observed with bees—and vice versa. This only shows how thoughtlessly these experiments were carried out.

Now, one can add the following: you see, when one proceeds further* to the so-called ultra-violet rays—here you have red-orange, yellow, green, blue—then indigo would come in, and the violet—the ultra-violet rays. On the other side, the infra-red rays.

We have here the ultra-violet rays (on the right hand side) and these have the peculiarity (so he himself expresses it in the article) that they produce strong chemical reactions. Whatever is introduced *here* (into the sphere of the ultra-violet light) is strongly affected chemically, with the result that if I now put an ant here it will at once experience a strong chemical reaction. It feels this; that is true. It feels this effect above all in the eyes. When the ant is brought into the sphere of the ultra-violet rays it feels this, just as barium platino-cyanide reacts when brought into the same sphere of chemical activity. If I completely darken a room and have only the ultra-violet rays there, then the ant would notice at once that something was happening. For instance, if one had ants' eggs or larvae they would be completely changed, they would be destroyed the moment this powerful chemical working occurred. This is why the ants rescue their eggs.

What this article is really concerned with is effects of a chemical nature.

The statement I made recently is quite correct. I said the bees have a sense which is intermediate between smell and taste; thus these things are sensed by the bees, and it is similar in the case of ants. So little are these gentlemen aware of the real question that they do not know, for example, that when man himself perceives colours, even in perceiving the ultra-violet rays, slight chemical changes take place in his eyes. Man's perception of colour tends to be of a chemical nature.

All that has been investigated here is the reaction to the inner chemical change that takes place in the bees when they are in the ultra-violet light.

Now all that is within the sphere of black, white, yellow, grey (and grey is only a somewhat darker white), or blue-grey, in all these colours there is no ultra-violet. Thus all these colours are freely perceptible to the bees. The chemical effects which the bees sense so strongly when they come to the ultra-violet are not present in these colours. But when the bee leaves the sphere of black, white, yellow and blue-grey and comes into this other sphere it feels in the ultra-violet rays something alien to it. There the bee can do nothing. It is thus so important to note that the bee has a sense between taste and smell.

We men make a great distinction between smell and taste. The latter is primarily a chemical sense; it is entirely based on

---

*(drawing on the black-board.)

chemistry. The bee has something which is intermediate between taste and smell. This does not contradict the fact that the bee is able to distinguish colour when the front of the hive is painted in one way or another; for you must consider that as all colours differ in their chemical effects, so they can also be perceived in relation to their warmth or coldness.

If, for example, you cover a surface with red paint and the bee approaches it, it experiences warmth. How should the bee not know that this is different from coming, for instance, into the sphere of blue! Near the blue surface the bee senses coldness. The bee senses the warmth of red and the cold of blue, and then it can naturally distinguish between them. But one is not therefore justified in concluding that the bee sees with its eyes in the way man does. This of course is utter nonsense. But so it is with many other things that people think.

I have previously told you what all such experiments amount to. I once told you there is a certain plant, called the "Venus fly-trap" which immediately contracts its leaves when they are touched. Just as you make a fist of your hand when you are going to be touched—that is, when somebody means to give you a blow—so the Venus fly-trap waits for the insect and then shuts itself up. Then people say: this plant, the Venus fly-trap, has a soul like men have. It is aware of the arrival of the insect and shuts itself up.

Yes, gentlemen, but I always say: I know of a certain arrangement so constituted that when an animal approaches it and touches something inside it, then it immediately shuts up and the animal is caught. This is a mouse-trap! If one ascribes a soul to the Venus fly-trap, one must equally ascribe one to the mouse-trap! If one ascribes sight to the bees because they do something or other in ultra-violet light, then one ought to ascribe sight to barium platino-cyanide as well!

If people only took the trouble to think they would discover many quite remarkable things, for barium platino-cyanide consists of barium. This is a white metal belonging to the class of alkaline metals. Now it is interesting that such metals play a certain part in the life of man. As human beings we could not have the right working in our bodies of the albumen we take in if we had not such metals in our pancreas. They must be there. In *barium* we have something connected with our feeling comfortable in our digestive process. *Platinum* is an especially valuable metal, as you know; a metal that is also especially hard and heavy—it is a precious metal. All these metals have the property that they are, once more connected with feeling, with "sensing."

Now remind yourselves of another thing. *Cyanide* is also there. This is a certain kind of cyanic acid, of prussic acid. I told you before that man always develops a little prussic acid in the working of his muscles. This substance thus resembles what man is constantly producing in his body. You can gather from this that man is particularly susceptible in his body—not in his eyes—to what happens in ultra-violet light—*i.e.*, to the chemical components of light. We can judge for ourselves if we only pay attention to these things.

But it is only Spiritual Science that can enable one to observe such matters as the fact that where barium platinocyanide is affected a kind of feeling arises. This applies to the bees in the highest degree. The bees sense colours with especial intensity, but they only *see* the colours dimly shining on the appearance of a self-luminous organism.

For this reason I say, that generally speaking, twilight surrounds the bees. But when the new Queen appears, she shines for the other bees as the glow-worms shine for us when June is here. This is so, only as regards the three small frontal eyes; the other eyes, the larger ones, have already some perception of light, but as in twilight. When it is in darkness the creature senses the presence of just those colours that work chemically, such as ultra-violet, or of one that does not work chemically at all—*i.e.*, the infra-red.

At the end of this article in the bee journal, it is stated that further information as to the infra-red rays will be given later. Certainly, when the bees come to the infra-red, they will behave quite differently, for then there are no longer any chemical effects.

As to the facts, the experiments are correct, but one must be clear that one cannot draw conclusions such as Forel and Kühn have actually done. To do so is a totally thoughtless way of following up the experiments. Then people say: "this has been proved beyond contradiction." Naturally, but only for those who ascribe a soul to the mouse-trap! But for others who know how far one can go, how far one is able to think in such a way that things are rightly followed up, these proofs are by no means beyond contradiction.

In ordinary life we are not in the habit of following things up accurately. When people experience some small matter or another, then, as the saying is, a gnat can become an elephant. And so it is with our scientists. When they get hold of something they don't stop their thinking, but carry it on, and apply it to what is immediately before them. This results in fantastic nonsense; a gnat becomes an elephant. When modern science makes such statements this is due to its authority, for what is thus brought forward meets, as a rule, with no contradiction, because all the periodicals are in the hands of scientific authorities. But in the long run, one will not be able to make much use of this nonsense.

If you go over the whole ground of bee-keeping, I believe you will find that just the very best bee-keepers do not trouble themselves very much about the discoveries of Forel and Kühn; for bee-keepers must work practically, and then instinctively one does what is necessary. Of course, it is best if one has the right instincts. I seem to have noticed that the bee-keeper sometimes likes to settle down on a Sunday evening, when it is snowing perhaps, and to read some such article, because naturally, it interests him, but he cannot make much out of it because in an article of this kind there is nothing he can get hold of.

But surely, gentlemen, you have other interesting things to ask me about?

HERR MULLER:

I should like to add something about the Queen. We have already described how she lays her eggs. Then we have the unfertilised Queens; for instance, in bad weather, and then only drones are hatched which have no value. Also, when a Queen dies and there is no young brood, then one of the worker bees is bred to be a Queen. It also lays eggs but only unfertilised eggs, from which only inferior drones come out.

2. Then I should like to add something about swarming. At the time of the first swarm there is as yet no new Queen there. She is still asleep in her cell and cannot yet provide new brood. Only the older bees leave the hive with the Queen. I can take her out and put the whole swarm back in the hive.

3. As to the sight of the bees, I should like to say that when we are at work in the bee-house and there is too much light there (for the bee-master himself there is always too little light), then the bees are terribly agitated.

As to stinging when the bees are swarming, it is well known with us that the first swarm is rather ticklish; this is much less the case with casts, We hold the opinion that young bees do not sting, that they do not use their stings.

4. There are certain districts where people do not harvest the honey before August 8, which is held to be a Holy day. August 8 is a honey day.

5. It can happen that the swarm goes out and the Queen settles somewhere, and it seems that is an end of it, but it is not so—not altogether so.

DR. STEINER:

With regard to what I said, everything pointed to the fact that the old Queen leaves the hive when the new Queen shows herself and appears to the bees like a glow-worm. When the swarm goes out and the old Queen has been captured, then one can return all the bees into the hive, as you say, and they will go on working quietly. That does not mean that one cannot therefore say that the bees were first driven out by the strong effect of the light of the new Queen on their tiny eyes. This cannot be done away with. You must proceed quite logically here. I will give you an example from life. Imagine for a moment, that all of you here were employed somewhere, and you discover one day that you must all go on strike because something is wrong with the management. Let us suppose you all decide to go on strike. So you swarm out, gentlemen.

Then a certain time passes and you find yourselves unable to procure the necessities of life. You reach the hunger-stage, and are obliged to go back to your work. I cannot now say that therefore you had originally no reason to run away! You must consider that if you take the old Queen out of the swarm and bring her back into the hive, then naturally, the bees must endure the new Queen after all, for the old Queen is no longer there. They must bite into the sour apple! What I said is therefore not wrong; it is a question of seeing these things in the right light.

Then you spoke about the first swarm, when the new Queen is not yet there, when you cannot yet speak of her. Well, have you ever seen a first swarm when even the egg of the Queen is not there?

HERR MULLER:

Nine days before the young Queen has crept out.

DR. STEINER:

To begin with the young Queen is within her cell, as an egg. After sixteen days she is a full-grown Queen; then she creeps out. *Nine days* before this she is already there in the egg. The strange thing is that the *egg* shines brightest of all. Gradually it shines less and less, but the young Queen still shines for some time; she shines strongest of all in the larval state. Thus, it is quite comprehensible that you may have several swarms made up of the most sensitive of the bees which go out. It is to be explained by the fact that nothing happens before the young Queen is there. For what is the young Queen? She is already there when only the egg is there.

As to an unfecundated Queen, when the Queen is not fertilised then no worker-bees come out but only drones, and as Herr Müller said, very bad drones at that. This is true. The brood of an unfertilised Queen is useless because there are no worker-bees. One must see to it that the Queen can make her nuptial flight under the influence of the Sun.

You see, gentlemen, once more, what a great part is played by the chemical element. For what takes place on this flight is an effect on the sexual nature of the bee. But the sexual nature is entirely of a chemical character. When the Queen flies so high then naturally the impregnation is not brought about by the light, but by the chemical working of the light. Just in this instance you can see how delicately sensitive the bee is to the chemical element.

You said further that while at work in the bee-house, as a man one naturally needs light, and this makes the bees restless.

Try to form a vivid picture of the bee receiving chemical reactions from the light which it feels terribly strongly. When you, as a human being, approach and let the light in, suddenly making it light everywhere, this affects the bee as a strong gust of air affects you; it is just as if you opened the window and a strong draught were to blow in. The bee *senses* the light, it does not feel that it becomes light all round it, but it senses the light as a concussion, it is quite shattered by it. One could almost say, (though I have not actually seen the bee-keeper letting in too much light) the bees become terribly nervous, inwardly restless. They are thrown into these chemical workings of the light and begin to fly hither and thither almost like little swallows. They dance up and down as a sign of how restless they feel within.

The bees would not behave in such a highly nervous way if they could *see* the light; they would then try to hide away, to creep into a corner where the light could not thus affect them.

Naturally, in all these matters, we must realise how perfectly clear we need to be as to effects that everywhere exist, and must not be compared with the effects things have upon men. Otherwise we anthropomorphise everything, and cannot but conclude that because man sees in a certain way, the animals also must do the same. One cannot make such statements straightaway.

Maybe you have observed the following. If one notices such things, one can often become aware of them. Imagine you are in a kitchen where the stove is nice and warm. The cat likes to sit on the warm stove; it curls itself up and falls asleep, has its eyes shut. Well, if there is a mouse somewhere under the cupboard, which the cat cannot possibly see with its eyes, it may happen that the cat suddenly springs down without opening its eyes, pounces with absolute certainty on the mouse, and before you have time to think the thing out to the end, the cat returns with the mouse already in its mouth.

Now naturally, you gentlemen, will not say the cat *saw* the mouse, for it had its eyes shut, it was asleep. Some people say the cat has a very fine sense of hearing, and by means of this very sensitive hearing the cat is aware of the mouse. Well, apart from this, that one must now state that the cat hears best when it is asleep, which is a rather doubtful statement, because sight and hearing are those senses which play so great a part in waking life, whereas the sense of smell for example, plays an extremely important part in sleep. It works chemically. Within the nose, and the whole brain something chemical is happening. Moreover, when you hear something, can you pounce upon it with absolute certainty? This is not at all the case; hearing is not at all such that it leads one to orientate oneself quickly. Hence, it is not the hearing of the cat that is in question here. But what is very strongly present in the cat is a terribly fine sense of *smell*, which it has within its bristly beard. This terribly fine sense of smell is there because in each bristle there is a little channel, and within each bristle (see diagram 9) is a substance, and this substance is chemically affected by the presence of the mouse. When there is no mouse near, this substance has a certain chemical quality, but if there is a mouse anywhere in the neighbourhood of the cat, even some distance away, then the the cat is aware of the mouse through the chemical reaction in its whiskers.

I told you once that there are people who, though living on the third floor, are aware of some substance in the cellar, and can sometimes be made ill by it—for example, by buckwheat.

People could easily convince themselves with what certainty the sense of smell works, for otherwise there could be no police dogs. These dogs work very little by sight, but much with their sense of smell. In the animal kingdom precision and sureness cannot be ascribed to the eyes, but to *chemical activity*; under the influence of ultra-violet rays this activity is strongest of all.

If you wished to be especially gracious to a police dog you would do well if, for instance, you went with him and constantly held a dark lantern in front of him so that you kept him always in the ultra-violet rays. The police dog would then be even more certain in finding things, for in its "smelling hairs" (for the dog also has smelling hairs) the chemical reactions would be still more certain.

All that can be known about the animal points to the fact that the moment we enter the animal kingdom, one must not look for such conscious senses as those of man, but must descend into the senses of smell and taste—into the "chemical senses."

You indicated, Herr Müller, that young bees do not sting. This is easily accounted for, for young bees have not yet the organ of the sting as they have not fully developed their whole inner organisation. This comes only as they grow older. There is nothing especially remarkable in this, and it does not contradict what I have said.

(Herr Müller asked about artificial feeding. He takes for this four parts of water, five of sugar, and then adds thyme, camomile-tea and a pinch of salt. What is the effect of this?)

DR. STEINER:

We are especially able to give you information in this matter, because our own remedies are partly based on the same principles as those that have been used instinctively here. Not all our remedies, but a certain number of them, are founded on similar principles.

You see, when you feed the bees on sugar, this is certainly nonsense, for the natural food of the bees is not sugar but nectar or honey, and pollen.

HERR MULLER:

For example, one has to empty even the half-filled combs of honey that come from the woods, because otherwise the bees get dysentery; also when the bees have at times only 4—6 lbs., left over, this is not sufficient.

DR. STEINER:

Bees are not accustomed to feed on sugar but on nectar and honey. This is in accordance with their whole nature. The remarkable thing here is that in winter the bee changes whatever food it happens to get into a kind of honey. All food is changed by the creature that partakes of it. Thus, in winter the bee is able, in its delicate digestive processes, to transform the food it takes into a kind of honey.

You can well imagine that this is a proceeding demanding much stronger forces than when you feed the bees on honey. They do not then need to expend the same amount of strength as when they must change sugar into honey. What kind of bees then will those be which within themselves can transform sugar into honey? They will only be the strongest bees, of which one can make good use. One cannot get weak bees to change sugar into honey; hence, they are more or less useless.

Now I said just now that we can well understand why you take for example, camomile tea, because you thereby spare the bee something which it has otherwise to do in its own body. If you dilute the sugar with camomile tea, then you take that part of the plant which prepares the nectar. For the substance of the camomile tea has not only camomile in it, for every plant also contains potential honey (the camomile contains this process in a greater degree, and can for this reason not be used as a honey plant). Suppose you have a plant, with a great deal of so-called starch in it. The starch has a constant tendency to change into sugar. The camomile sap already works on the starch of the plant in such a way that it directs the sugar-sap of the plant towards the formation of nectar.

If you give the bees camomile tea you support them in their inner honey-process. You make the sugar already like honey, when you dilute it with camomile tea. We do the same with our remedies. When one takes some kind of metal, one cannot give it to a human being just as it is, because it would disappear in the course of digestion. You must dilute it with something so that it can be more readily absorbed, and so it is with the camomile tea which you add to the sugar. Salt must be added for the reason that salt especially makes otherwise indigestible things, digestible.

Man instinctively puts salt into his soup, because salt has the property of spreading rapidly through the body, and makes food digestible.

LECTURE IV.

Dornach, December 1, 1923.

HERR MÜLLER has handed me another number of the "*Swiss Bee-keeper's Journal*" with an article dealing with the results of certain experiments with honey-cures—("Our further Experiences with Honey-cures in the Frauenfeld Children's Home, Amden," by Dr. Paula Emrich. Weeson. (No III of the "*Schweizerische Bienenzeituna*" March 1923). (Certain passages from this article were read aloud).

DR. STEINER:

It will be quite interesting, gentlemen, to add today a few remarks on this article. In this Children's Home an attempt was made to give honey treatments to children found to be suffering from some form or other of mal-nutrition. As described here, the treatment was to dissolve the honey and stir it well into moderately warmed milk, not brought to boiling point but kept just below it. This mixture was given to the children.

Excellent results were thus attained. The author, Dr. Paula Emrich, mentions the satisfactory result that the percentage of red corpuscles in the blood of these children increased to an extraordinarily high degree. For instance, two children were admitted belonging to the same family. On arrival the younger child had only 53% of red blood-corpuscles. On leaving, after a honey-treatment, the percentage had risen to 82%. The elder child had at first 70%, and on leaving this had risen to 78%. In this case there was thus less improvement, but still some improvement.

The elder child had milk only, and benefitted by it, but the percentage rose only from 70% to 78%; it was therefore, to begin with, not so weakly, but did not get stronger in the same proportion.

There are still quite a number of very interesting experiments. As I shall refer to them, I should like to ask you to note carefully the ages of the children concerned. If one is to observe the effects of some special substance on a person, it is no use simply to make experiments in the laboratory; one has always first to find out the age of every patient; one must always note the age in any experiments in nutrition, or in healing.

Here we have a boy aged 11; he went through a honey-cure lasting 8 weeks, with the result of a very considerable improvement in his glands. A case of cattarrh of the upper parts of the lungs also improved, the red corpuscles—those really significant elements—increasing from 55% to 75%.

Then again we have a boy aged 11. He shows a rise from

50% to 74%. Then a girl aged 11, with a rise from 70% to 88%. The rise is throughout, significant. She then gives the increase in weight also, which shows that the children became stronger. I will not read the further details.

Mention is also made of a girl aged 10, of another of the same age; then a boy aged 13, a girl of 7, a boy aged 11, a boy aged 8, a boy of 12, a boy of 9 and a boy of 7.

The experiments show that children of these ages, let us say roughly, the school-age, derive great benefit from a honey-cure.

Now, this doctor tries to discover why the children benefitted so remarkably from this treatment with honey. And here, gentlemen, he mentions something very interesting, something which in a most remarkable way condemns what is so largely applied in science today.

For what does science do now-a-days when it tests food-stuffs in respect to their nutritive value? Science analyses certain food-substances to discover how many components of one or another chemical substance are to be found in it. This is what science does.

Now the following thing happened—a pupil of the famous Bunge, the Professor of Physiology—(you very probably know him by name, he was at one time in Basel)—made experiments in feeding mice with milk. These mice had a good time of it, they throve extremely well when they were fed on milk. So now he made the experiment in another way. He said:—milk consists of casein—*i.e.* cheese-substance, fat, sugar and salts. He said to himself:—the mice throve splendidly on milk; milk consists of casein, fat, sugar and salts; consequently, I shall give some mice casein, fat, sugar and salts. This is exactly what is contained in milk. And behold! when he gave the mice casein, fat, sugar and salts, they died within a few days! They got the same things, but they all died.

You see, gentlemen, the composition of the substance is not the whole matter. Those gentlemen ought to have said to themselves: something else must be in question here. But what did they say? They said: "substance is everything: substance must be everywhere where anything happens."

Well, yes, but the substances that are there in casein, fat, sugar and salts—well, they do not make *milk*. So the gentlemen said, evidently there must be a new substance here, in such minute quantities that it cannot be found by chemical analysis. This substance is what people now call—*vitamin*. *Vita* means *life*; *min* is connected with "*make*"; therefore, *vitamin* "*makes life.*"

Once, gentlemen, when Heine wanted to mock at something, he said: "There are people who wish, for instance, to explain poverty, the cause of poverty. Well, the simplest way is to say—'*poverty comes from being poor!*'" One has found another term, but one has not explained anything! I was once in a society where people discussed the question where what is "comic" came from. Some of them had arrived at quite interesting ideas as to the source of the "comic"—of what one laughs at. Then however, someone got up and went to the platform in a way that one knew at once—"he has the feeling he has a great deal to say." So then he brought forward his ideas of "comic" and said:— "The 'comic' originates solely from the fact that man possesses a 'vis-comica.' 'Vis' is *force*—'comica' is *comic*. Man has the 'comic force.' This is where what is 'comic' originates."

This is just as though one should say in economics:—where does money come from? Money comes from the money-making-force. Nothing is explained in this way. Well—in economics one would at once remark that anyone saying that money comes from the money-making-force was a queer fellow! But in science people do not notice it when someone asks:—where does the life-giving property of milk come from? and then answers:—from the vitamin! That is the same as saying that poverty comes from being poor! But it is not noticed. People think they have said something wonderful, but in truth nothing at all has been said. And that, you see, is what I should like to call the disturbing element in modern scientific methods. People claim to have something to say; they announce it in gigantic words, and everybody believes what is said. But if this continues further in the history of the world, things will come to a point where everything will dry up and perish. For the world depends on the fact that *something can be done*, not that things are merely discussed and many words made about them. Words must signify what is there in reality.

And truly, gentlemen, in earlier times a kind of knowledge existed that was directly connected with practise. Today there is a science which no longer knows anything about practical matters. Often it merely spins out words. This has naturally come about because a new authority has superseded an old authority.

You need only consider how short a time ago it is that we did not have so many journals on special subjects as we have today. Communications which were to be made on various subjects—let us say for instance bee-keeping—were given out at special bee-keepers' meetings. This was still so in my youth. At such a gathering of bee-keepers one could learn how things were being dealt with. One would tell the other what he knew from his own experience, and one felt at once whether a man was merely a wind-bag, or whether he had real practical knowledge behind him, which is a very different matter. When you hear someone speak, you know at once whether he knows something, or whether you can find it all in print somewhere. For printer's ink has come as a new authority in addition to all the rest. If anything is printed people believe there must be something in it!

But there is something further to be considered in this article. This doctor has indeed achieved something of great value with her honey treatments. What she has done in her practical work is really admirable. But when she begins to think it all over on scientific lines, the result is really nil. Further she says this:—

"It is much to be desired that these results of our experiments should be made known as widely as possible, and that more honey should be given, especially to the young . . . . For the moment our communications only give the results of our practical experiences; but we do not doubt that with the further development of the theory of vitamins the pharmacologists and physiologists will give their attention to the problem of the working of honey on the human organism."

The author also says at the beginning: "I feel obliged to give this account of the effects of honey-cures from the medical point of view. Our good results encourage us to seek their deeper connections, as I am well aware that I am far from having penetrated their innermost nature."

It is evident from her own words that this doctor is modest enough to admit that the whole theory of vitamins does not enable her to reach the real heart of the matter.

And now let us consider very exactly the following question. Let us see on what these effects of honey-treatments really rest. You see, these experiments show us something; they show that the effect of honey is an especially strong one, and that further experiments will increasingly show this, not in the case of very young children, but with those who have reached the change of teeth, or with those who are well beyond it. This is shown by the actual experiments, and it is extremely important to take this into account.

But the experiments indicate something further. They indicate that honey is most effective when one gives it in moderately heated milk. It is this admixture of milk and honey that has such especially favourable results with children. If one went a little further one would discover that honey is important even in the case of the younger children. One must then put only a little honey in the milk— more milk and less honey. With old people it is the honey without any milk that is good. Excellent results can be obtained with really old people if one persuades them to to take honey without milk. We must say that milk and honey have very great importance in human life; these experiences make it evident.

You see, the old wisdom, as I have often told you, was not so stupid as modern learning thinks. This old wisdom is sometimes expressed in very simple words, but it was really wise. In the ancient saying:—"This is a land where milk and honey flow," the meaning is that it is a land of health, a country where men can live healthily. Thus, of old, men knew that milk and honey have a tremendously strong relation to human life.

Nature often speaks in a very reasonable way. One observes her utterances if only one takes simple matters sufficiently simply.

If one knows that Nature works with great wisdom, one does not need much proof of the fact that milk is good for little children, for were it not so, honey would flow from the breasts of women and not milk. This would by no means be beyond the sphere of Nature's possibilities, for the plants produce honey and it certainly might be possible that the glands of the female breast secreted honey. One must only take things simply enough. One must not say:—Nature is a bungler, she makes only milk to flow from the woman's breast and not honey, but one must say:—Behind this lies the knowledge that for the small child, milk above all else is necessary; one can add the honey as the child grows older.

Well, then, surely we should not form such an idea as the above, which is nothing but mere words, and say to ourselves;—" poverty comes from being poor; the comical from the vis-comica, and the life-giving power of honey from the vitamin!" One must look for what has reality in this connection.

We will now, gentlemen, gather together some of the things we have long learnt to know from these lectures, for the important thing is that one should always observe things in the right way.

When you go into the mountains you find, just where the rocks are hardest, where so to speak, the very hardest earthly substance pours in—there you find the quartz-crystals. They are very beautiful. You find many kinds of crystals. You will remember I drew these quartz crystals for you; they look like this:—(Diagram 10). When they are entire, they are formed below just as they are above, but usually, they are not perfect. They come out of the rock; they grow, as it were, out of the rock in the form I have just drawn for you here. What does this signify?

It signifies that the earth permits crystals to grow out of itself which are *hexagonal*, growing to a point. Within the earth there is thus the power to build up this six-angled form.

As I have so often explained to you, the forces that are within the earth and in the universe, are also in man. The earth in her turn receives this force from the universe; man has it from the earth. Man has the same force within him which, in the earth, drives out the crystal. How is it then within him? Truly, gentlemen, the human body is full of quartz.

Quartz as you find it in the mountains is one of the very hardest of substances. But substances are not everywhere just as they present themselves to us here or there. In man there is something quite similar to quartz, but it is in a more fluid form. Why?

You see, if one observes—and one must really observe in the right way, and with a true inner vision—what flows continually from man's head into his limbs (see Diagram 11), and this is most interesting, there streams incessantly downwards from the head what the earth once upon a time caused to flow from within outwards, and which became hard up above there, and settled down, for instance, as quartz crystals. It streamed out from the interior of the earth. In man it flows from his head through the whole of his body. It is quartz, or silicic acid. But the human body does not permit the quartz to become a crystal. That would indeed be a fine business if we were all to be filled up inside with quartz crystals!

Only to a point where the quartz is about to become hexagonal does man allow the thing to go; there he stops it; he does not allow it to go any further. Thus we have only the beginnings of the quartz formation in our body, and then it is arrested; it must come to an end.

Our whole life rests on this—that we are perpetually on the point of forming hexagonal crystals from the head downwards, but we do not permit it actually to come about. These hexagonal crystals always wish to take form in us, but in reality they do not do so. They are interrupted, arrested, and then we have, so to speak, the quartz fluid in the highest possible state of solution within us.

If we had not this quartz-fluid within us, we could for example, eat ever so much sugar and we should never have a sweet taste in our mouth. This tasting of the sugar is brought about by the quartz we have within us, not by its substantiality, but by what is the *will* within it to become hexagonal like a crystal. That is what causes it; that is the essential.

You see, in the interior of the earth this crystalising process is continued. Man arrests the silicic acid when it wants to grow spiky up above inside him. The earth allows it to become spiky up above.

But man needs this force, this silicic acid force—*i.e.*, this power to bring forth hexagonal forms—man has need of it.

I imagine that you are not all of you good geometricians. Geometry is not exactly familiar to you all; you could perhaps not straight away, draw a quartz crystal, or model one in clay. But your body is a very good geometrician, and wants always to be forming such crystals. We are prevented from doing this. All life consists in the holding back of death, and when we can no longer hold death back, we die.

Now let us look at the bees. The bee flies out and gathers nectar. This it works upon in its own body, and in so doing provides its own life-forces. Further the bee prepares the wax. What does it do with the wax? It makes hexagonal cells. You see, the earth makes hexagonal silicic-acid crystals. The bee makes hexagonal cells, and this is extremely interesting. If I could draw the bees' cells for you—or if you remember Herr Müller showing them to you—then they look just like quartz crystals, only they are hollow. But in their form they are the same.

You see, these cells are hollow (Diagram 12), but what is put in them? The bees' eggs are laid there. Where there is silicic acid in the quartz, here in the cell is a hollow, and there the bee places its eggs. The bee is shaped by the same force that is within the earth and forms the quartz. Here the finely dissolved silicic acid (Diagram 13) is at work. A force is at work there, though this cannot be physically proved. The nectar works in the body of the bee so that it can shape the wax in a form which man really needs, for man must have those six-cornered spaces within him. Man needs the same thing. Inasmuch as the bee is the creature best able to give form to this hexagonal force, the bee is the creature that everywhere collects that particular food which can best be transformed in the body into this hexagonal force.

You need only eat some honey and you receive an immensely strengthening force. If you are too weak to develop this hexagonal force in yourself which has to pass from the head into the whole body, if you no longer have the power to give the blood so much firmness that this force is always present in it, then honey must intervene—or milk in the case of the child. The child has not yet got this hexagonal force; therefore, it must receive it from what is prepared in the human being as milk.

Now you see, gentlemen, that you can give as much casein, fat, sugar and salts to the mice as you please— and they will die. Why? Because the animal also, needs this hexagonally-working force. If one only mixes together chemically casein, fat, sugar, and salts, then the force present in the hexagon is not there. When you give the mice *milk* then it is there. Only in milk it is not so strongly present that when the milk is turning sour it crystallises hexagonally. If this hexagonally-working force were a little stronger in milk, one could drink sour milk and it would form little silicic-acid crystals on the tongue. This would taste as though the milk were full of tiny little hairs. But it does not go so far, because milk comes from the human or animal body, and there it remains fluid. This is sufficient for the child but not for the grown man. But to become adult is something that already begins in childhood, so we must give the child the more powerfully-working hexagonal force that honey contains.

You see, gentlemen, it is very interesting that when you take milk, even if it comes from the human being, it is still something belonging to the animal-nature in man. In man it is animal. If you take honey, it comes from the plant kingdom—indirectly through the bee. But it comes from the plant world and has a plant nature. If you take silicic acid—quartz—then this has a mineral-nature; it has quite a definite hexagonal form. The wax which is produced within the bee itself through the food which is its nourishment, the wax has *received* its form; it does not originate it, it receives the form as developed in the hexagonal cell. In milk this form is dissolved again; only a shadow-picture of the hexagonal crystal remains in the milk (see Diagram 14). Thus, one can say that honey is a substance most suitable and health-giving for man.

One might however, be inclined to think that it would be just as good if man were to take some silicic acid instead of honey, for then he would also obtain this hexagonal force. But the silicic acid which has been driven as far as the hexagonal form, as far as to evolve this silicic acid form, contains too powerful a crystallising force; it would work much too strongly in man.

Now let us imagine the following. Picture to yourselves some poor child not so fortunate as to be given this honey-cure (as described in the article), at the age of 16 or 17, or at 13 or 14, when it is most suitable. This child has not had this good fortune and the iron-corpuscles in the blood get weaker and weaker.

The percentage in the blood gets less and less. The child grows up, let us say to the age of 30, and has grown up into a weak man. The writer of this article describes this also when she says, "they collapse." When the man is 30 years of age it may often be a very good thing to give him a honey-treatment, but he is already too much exhausted; he would have to eat so much honey to get any real benefit from it that his digestion would be ruined. Honey teaches man moderation; if you eat too much honey you ruin your stomach.

This rests on quite a simple fact. Honey is sweet; it contains a great deal of sugar. The stomach especially needs acids, and when you put too much sugar into the stomach you hinder the working of the acids. Thus, briefly put, honey must only be eaten in moderate quantities, and when a man is already exhausted at the age of 30, one would have to give him so much honey, if a honey-treatment was to help him (and this it would doubtless do), that he would first get bad stomach disturbances and then intestinal troubles. Thus, one cannot do this, but one can do something else. One can at first give the man very highly diluted, pulverised quartz, that is, silicic acid as a remedy. When you have given him this highly diluted silicic acid as a medicine for a time, then after a time he will be able to benefit by small quantities of honey. The strongly diluted silicic acid will have called forth in him the power to make use of the hexagonal force, and then a small amount of honey can follow. The silicic acid has prepared the way for the honey.

One might also help a man with whom the content of the blood in regard to hæmoglobin has become exhausted, by adding to the honey, suitable to an adult, some highly diluted silicic acid; the honey can then take effect. In the case of a child one should give plenty of milk.

You see, it is necessary to know these connections. One might ask: what then is it that works through the honey into man? It is the formative forces of the hexagonal principle. This is within the bees themselves. One can see it in the waxen cells of the comb, and it is this that makes honey so beneficial. It was for this reason that I said just now that it is primarily the force of milk that works in the child, and this can be further enhanced by the addition of honey, whereas in the adult person the forces of the honey are more especially active.

Nevertheless, when a man has grown older this honey force must be strengthened by that of silicic acid, as I told you. Also, a milk and honey cure can be of use because the forces of early childhood still exist in the older man; this is beyond contradiction; the good effect of a honey-cure remains undoubted.

In practise, this is well-known, and one should really insist on making these things so clear to people, that a right amount of good honey should be available. On this matter people are very readily deceived. I do not mean this in a bad sense; I might say people are easily mislead by the conditions of present day civilisation. If you have ever asked for honey in hotels when travelling, it was certainly not honey that you were given there, it was sugar-honey, artificially produced.

If people realised that this is by no means the same thing, for there can be no question of any hexagonal force being in such honey, they would never claim that imitation-honey could have the same effect as pure bee-honey. One could very well feed mice with pure honey, they would like it very well. But if you were to feed them on this artificial honey, they would die, though not perhaps in a few days. I have now added what I wished to say about this article on milk and honey cures.

Now another interesting question has been put to me about which I would like to speak, and also to hear what you yourselves have to say about it; also what Herr Müller has to say to you. You see, there are so many matters to be considered that it will really be worth our while to discuss these things further next time. You will then be able to ask your questions, and Herr Müller or I will answer them.

I want first to touch quite briefly on two other points. They may seem rather strange to you, but I am really eager to know what you will have to say about them.

WRITTEN QUESTION:

Among old-fashioned bee-masters there is a conviction that a certain soul-relationship exists between the bee-master and his bees. It is said that when the bee-father dies, then his death must be at once announced to all the bees. If this is not done, then the whole stock will die out in the course of the following year. That a certain relationship of soul does exist between the two is again indicated by the fact that one gets far more stung when one approaches one's work in the hive in an angry or irritable mood, then when one does the same work in a peaceful and harmonious one. Is there any objective reality at the base of this old idea of the bee-masters?

DR. STEINER:

It would be interesting if Herr Müller would tell us quite simply whether he believes such things to be quite in the air or no? Such things are customary among the peasant bee-keepers; they announce a death to the bees. But this soul-relationship, this connection between the bee-father and his bees, is what I now have in mind. Perhaps Herr Müller can tell us more.

HERR MULLER:

Two cases were cited which had occurred in Basel and in Zürich. In one family a woman who had helped a good deal with the bees had died, and in the course of a year all the bees were dead. In the other case, at Basel, it was also a woman who died who had given much care to the bees; the same thing happened. It was a very large apiary; in a year's time twenty-eight stocks were reduced to six. One cannot explain this by anything connected with the general conditions, or with the bees themselves. One could trace any disease that the bees may have had. It may have been a "soul" connection.

DR. STEINER:

Let us remember what I once told you about the relation

between man and the animals. You may perhaps have heard, gentlemen (I have spoken of it before), that some time ago people talked a great deal about the so-called "counting" horses, horses which, for instance, were asked the question: "How much is four and five?" Then one counted— 1, 2, 3, 4, 5, 6, 7, 8, 9—and the horse stamped its foot at nine. Really remarkable and not inconsiderable sums were done in this way—by the horses. You may perhaps have heard of these "Elberfeld counting horses"; they were very celebrated. Whole delegations went to investigate the matter.

I did not myself see these horses, but I saw another horse belonging to Herr von Osten that could count equally well. One could form an exact judgment of the whole matter. People simply racked their brains over these "counting horses," for it is naturally something fundamentally terrible that horses should suddenly begin to count. Science itself was put to shame by such a thing! Naturally one was quite aware, for it is an obvious conclusion to reach, that a horse cannot count; one had to find out how it was that the horse stamped its foot at a correct number. In reality, it cannot count; it would be quite idiotic to think a horse could count. Even a University lecturer knew this who scientifically investigated the matter, but he constructed a theory. He said: "Herr von Osten makes a slight facial movement when he counts; the horse observes the lines in his face, and in response to those it stamps its foot." But he himself then made the following objection: "Yes," he said, "but in that case the horse should be standing in front of Herr von Osten, and be looking at him, observing his face so that it knows when to stamp." So he then took this position himself and saw nothing. Still, he did not give up his theory, he merely said: "The change of face is so minute that I cannot perceive it, but the horse can!"

Well gentlemen, it then follows that a horse can see more than a University lecturer! Nothing else can be inferred!

The matter was naturally otherwise. If one is trained by spiritual science and then observes the facts, one does not then lay much stress on some small facial change, for it happened in this way: there on the one side stood the horse; there stood Herr von Osten, very lightly holding the bridle. In his right hand waistcoat pocket Herr von Osten had plenty of sugar. Now Herr von Osten perpetually gave the horse little lumps of sugar. The horse licked them, found them sweet, and loved Herr von Osten very dearly. It loved him ever more and more through these little lumps of sugar, and thus an affectionate relation was set up between the horse and Herr von Osten. The latter had no need to make faces, he had merely to *think*—nine is the correct number; then the horse could *sense* it, for animals have a most delicate perception for what is going on around them. They *sense* what is going on there inside man's head even if he indulges in no small grimaces which a horse might be able to see but not a man. The horse *senses* what is happening when the brain *thinks—nine—*and then it stamps. But if the horse had not had any sugar its love would be a little changed into hate, and it would not have stamped with its foot any more.

Thus, you see, the animal has a very delicate perception of things; not of little grimaces, but of things actually not visible; for instance, with the horse, this sensing of what is going on in the brain of Herr von Osten. One has only to observe the facts, and then one knows how wonderful a sensitiveness the animals have.

Just imagine for a moment that you go near a number of bees, and are very much afraid of them. The bees will feel this fear in you, that is undeniable. Well, what does it mean when one is afraid? When one is afraid of something or other one grows pale, fear makes people pale. When one turns pale the blood flows inwards, it does not go outwards into the skin. When the bee comes near a man who is afraid, it senses more than it normally does when the blood is in the skin. It senses the hexagonal force of the blood, and stings into it; it would like to get honey or wax from you. On the other hand, when a man works quietly and his blood is flowing evenly in his veins, then the bee senses something quite different.

And now think of a man who is angry, and in his anger he goes to the bees. Anger makes a man red, and a great deal of blood flows into the skin, for the blood would absorb the hexagonal force. This, too, the bee senses in its delicate feeling and believes you would deprive it of this force—and it stings you. So fine are the subtle sensibilities of the forces of nature at work here.

And now we come to the question of habit. Think of the bee-father, the bees do not see his approach as men would do, the bee "senses"—if I may use this expression—everything that emanates from him—how all this is constituted. The bees get used to this, and should the bee-father die they must re-adjust themselves, and this means a great deal to them.

And now, for a moment, think what one finds even with dogs when the master dies. It has been known to happen that the dog will go to the grave and die there, because it cannot adjust itself to a new master. Why should one suppose that the bee with its fine sensitiveness should not be aware of what happens, why should one not think that the bee also, accustomed as it is to the bee-master cannot at once adapt itself to a new one? Indeed something very significant lies at the root of all this.

But you may say: "Is it then the same with these tiny little creatures as with dogs and horses?" Well, perhaps you may not have noticed, but it is nevertheless true, that one finds men who have, as the saying is, a specially lucky hand in the cultivation of plants. Even when they sow plants, or grow flowers in a pot, everything thrives with them, while another person may take equal care of the plants, but none will thrive; he is not successful. This is due to the "emanations" man has, and which work favourably on the plants in the one case, and unfavourably in the other. It is quite impossible for some people to cultivate plants. They have an unfavourable reaction which above all affects the forces in the flower that produce nectar, the forces that sweeten the flower. So we can say, Man works even on the flowers, and in a much more pre-eminent way upon the bees.

One need not wonder at this, but one must bring the facts before one as they appear; then one begins to understand that things really are so, and can bring them to bear in practical life.

QUESTION:

According to an old peasant rule it is held that if it rains on the third of May, the Day of the Finding of the Holy Cross, the honey is washed out of all the flowers and trees, and there will be no good honey harvest that year. My observations of the last four years seem to confirm that there is some truth in this rule. Is such a thing at all possible?

DR. STEINER:

This question leads us very deeply into the great processes of Nature. You see, it is just this day of the Finding of the Holy Cross, this third of May which is of less importance; it is of much greater importance that it is just this season of the year. What does it actually mean when it rains at the beginning of May? It means this. You know that on March 23, the Sun enters the Sign of the Fishes. I have told you before that the spring equinox is now in this Sign of the Fishes. The Sun remains in this Sign till April 20, then it passes on into the Sign of the Ram. Thus the rays of the Sun come at the beginning of May from an entirely different corner of the Universe than at other times.

Suppose now that it is fine weather in the beginning of May— on the third of May—what does this signify? It signifies that on the third of May the Sun has a powerful influence on all that is earthly. Whatever happens on the earth is under the influence of the Sun when the weather is fine.

What then does is mean when it rains on May the third— that is in the beginning of May? It means that the *earth* has the strongest forces, and hinders the influences of the Sun. This is immensely significant for the whole plant kingdom, for when the rays of the Sun come from the direction of the Ram, they can so work that their whole power is directed to the plants. Then the flowers can develop the sweet substance which is present in honey. Then the bees can make honey.

When, however, the earth has the greater power, when it rains at this season, the flowers cannot develop in the rays of the Sun which come from the Ram, but must await later events, or maybe even be altogether interrupted in what they have already developed. Then the flowers do not mature the nectar rightly and the bees find none.

A matter such as this only becomes comprehensible when we know that everything that happens on this earth is, as I have repeatedly told you, under the influence of the Cosmos, of all that is outside and beyond the earth. Rain means that the influences of the Sun are chased away. Fair weather means that the Sun forces can unfold in all their power. The question here is not that the power of the Sun comes only in a general way, from where we look up to it, but that it comes definitely from that part of the heavens where the Ram is. The forces of the Sun differ according to the particular corner of the heavens from which they come. This is not due to the Sun alone, but because as the Sun shines down upon the earth, behind it, in this instance, in the Cosmos stands the constellation of the Ram. What the Ram gives, the Sun first absorbs and then pours it forth again with its rays. Thus, it is quite different if the Sun sends its rays to the earth at the beginning of May, or at the end of May. In the beginning of May the full force of the Ram is working; by the end of the month the Sun is already in the Sign of the Bull. These forces of the Bull cannot work with the same strength on the plants, they tend to harden and dry up the plant, and this means above all that the plant is no longer able to mature the forces for honey-production.

Thus something has really come to light from these old peasant rules that has sound reason, and one should take note of it. Naturally, as I have previously said—the consciousness of these things has been lost, and we have fallen into superstitions, for when one is no longer able to distinguish things one may easily become superstitious. Then these old peasant rules are of about the same value as the saying: "If the cock crows on the dunghill the weather will change, or will remain as it was before!"

This does not apply however, to all these old rules, for many of them are based on deep wisdom, and this we should once more study. The peasants who have applied these rules have sometimes done very well! A deeper wisdom will also lead us to the point where we can once more make use of them.

LECTURE V.

Dornach, December 5, 1923.

HERR ERBSMEHL remarked that in modern bee-keeping the bee-master is primarily concerned with making a profit; it is the material side that has to be considered. In the "*Bienenzeitung*" (No. 10) it says:—" Honey is for the most part a luxury, and those who can afford to buy it can well pay a good price for it." An instance is then given of how a certain Balmesberger who was travelling in Spain, found a number of very healthy children in a bee-keeper's house, and how in answer to the question where he sold his honey, he replied: " Here are my customers." Here in Middle Europe we want to get as much profit as possible from our honey. An employer of many workmen must see that he gets as much as possible out of them, and the same also applies to the bees.

In the eleventh number, the further question is asked as to whether there was any truth in the matter when people thought that moonlight had an influence on the production of honey or nectar in the flowers.

HERR MULLER replied:

1. That Herr Erbsmehl can gather from the Journal that the bee-keeper in question was only working on a small scale, and did not sell his honey. Erbsmehl is evidently not aware what bee-keeping is in our days, and all the things connected with it so that one is obliged to keep accounts. If one does not reckon on making a profit out of it, as with other matters, one might just as well give it up.

Honey would never be available in the necessary quantities if one did not have recourse to artificial methods. One gets perhaps 4—8 pounds of honey and may need rather more than this to keep the stock in good condition. Then a bad year comes and one has not enough to last till April or May. One must help the stock that has sufficient vitality by artificial feeding—with sugar, camomile tea, thyme and a small seasoning of salt.

Then the hours which the bee-keeper spends in working are noted down quite exactly in a modern apiary—how much time the bee-keeper has given to it and so on. Let us say five and a half hours;—(the hour is reckoned at the rate of one franc or one franc, fifty)—thus a pound of honey costs seven francs. Then one must reckon with wear and tear; the combs get used up, and one must replace them. The whole enterprise should surely make a profit. But if the bee-keeper remains at the old standpoint, he does not get along. Herr Erbsmehl may be able to do so, but if I have a large stock, then I must reckon up and say to myself—I have already made a loss if I sell my honey at six francs. The American bee-keepers take exactly this view.

2. I myself, cannot understand that within the next eighty to a hundred years the whole stock of bees will die out. I really cannot understand what Dr. Steiner means by saying that within eighty to a hundred years bee-keeping will be endangered.

3. As to the second point—*i.e.*, what announcing the death of the bee-master to the bees, has to do with the bee-master, I have already stated that the greater part of the stock dies after the death of the person in charge. How it came about, I am quite unable to understand.

4. With regard to impure honey in hotels I would like to say that first-class hotels frequently buy American honey. When bees are fed on this honey, they die—and yet it is produced by bees.

5. As to stinging, sweat is the very worst thing; when you hear shrill buzzing sounds, it is advisable to stand still.

6. As to the question how far can a bee sting effect a man, I know of a case which I should like to mention. A strong man was stung by a bee. He cried out: " Hold me, I have been stung !" He was extremely sensitive to it. He was a man with slight heart trouble. Perhaps Dr. Steiner will tell us to what extent a bee-sting may be really dangerous.

For instance, it is said that three hornet stings will kill a horse. A little while ago I found a hornets' nest in my bee-house. I was taking away the brood. The hornets were such cowards they did not sting me in the dark; perhaps they might have done so out of doors.

DR. STEINER:

Let us go back to the recognition by the bees of their bee-master. I should like to add a few remarks that we may discuss these matters in a reasonable way.

You have formed an opinion that is naturally completely justified if you consider the thing intellectually. But now I should like to tell you this: imagine you have a friend, you came to know him, let us say, in the year 1915. This friend stays here in Europe and you go to America, returning in the year 1925. Your friend, let us suppose, is in Arlesheim. You come to Arlesheim, meet your friend and recognise him. But what has happened meanwhile? I have already described to you how the matter, the substance of the human body is completely changed after seven or eight years. There is then nothing at all left of it; so that your friend when you see him again after ten years' interval, has nothing of the old, actually nothing, of the substance you saw in him ten years ago. Yet you recognised him! When you look at a man externally, he certainly looks like a coherent mass, but if you were to see him through a big enough magnifying glass, you would then see the blood flowing through his head. Very well, this blood when you see it with the naked eye, or with a *small* magnifying glass—this blood looks *like blood*. But if you imagine a gigantic magnifying glass then what flows there as blood no longer has the same appearance; then it seems to consist of little "dots" which are like minute animals. But these little dots do not remain at rest, they vibrate continually. And when you watch this going on it has the strangest likeness to a mass of bees. When sufficiently magnified in his substances, man appears exactly like a mass of bees.

If we thoroughly examine the whole matter it must seem just as incomprehensible that one man should be able to recognise another after ten years (for not a single one of these small vibrating dots is any longer there). His eyes are quite different dots, quite different minute creatures are there, and yet one man recognises another again!

So you see, it is entirely unnecessary that it should be due to these minute creatures and plants of which we consist, that we are able to recognise one another, for it is the *whole man* who again recognises us. The colony is not only just so and so many thousands of bees, the whole host of bees is a whole and complete unitary being that recognises a man or does not recognise him. If you had a diminishing glass instead of a magnifying glass you would be able to gather all these bees together; you could then visualise them as united in the same way as a human muscle. It is just this fact that one has to bear in mind with bees—that one is not dealing with single individual bees but must consider them as a *whole*, as belonging together as *one whole*.

With the intellect alone this cannot be grasped; one must be able to visualise it as a whole. It is for this reason that the bee colony is so profoundly instructive; it completely refutes all our usual ideas. Our ideas really always tell us that things ought to be different. But the most marvellous things happen in the hive; not at all such as we think out with our reason.

That it should have a certain effect upon the bees when, for instance, through the death of the bee-master another has to take his place, is undeniable. Experience has shown it to be a fact. Those who have had to do with many apiaries, and not only with one, know this quite well.

I can tell you that bee-keeping in a variety of ways interested me extremely when I was a boy, though the economic side, the financial problem of bee-keeping did not interest me so much then as later, or today— because honey even in those days was very dear and my parents could not afford to buy any. We got all our honey from our neighbours as a gift, for Christmas or at other times, indeed we had so much given us that we had honey all the year round. Honey was given away in those days.

You see the economic problem was not of great interest to me because, as a boy I ate a terrible lot of honey, as much indeed as I wanted of the honey that was given us.

How could this be? Nowadays, under the same circumstances one could not get so much honey as a gift, but in those days the bee-keepers in the neighbourhood of my parents' home were mostly farmers, and honey was just a part of the general farm produce. This is quite a different matter, gentlemen, from starting bee-keeping as some of you do while living on the wages you earn. On a farm, bee-keeping goes on without one's paying much attention to it. The time it takes up is not considered, is not taken into account. On the farm this was always so, it was time that remained over. Time was saved somewhere or other, or a bit of work was put off till another time and so on. At all events the honey was looked after between-whiles, and one had the idea that honey is something so precious that one cannot really pay for it at all.

In a certain sense this is quite right, but at the present time conditions are such that all price levels are quite false. It is fundamentally impossible to discuss prices today, for the whole question ought to be discussed on a much wider basis, on the basis of economics. Nothing much results if one discusses the price of separate food substances, and honey is a food substance, not merely a luxury or a pleasure. In a healthy social order a healthy price for honey would naturally be found; this is undoubted.

But because we do not live under healthy social conditions at the present day, all our problems are placed in an unhealthy position. When you visit big farms today and hear what the farm-bailiff has to say (as a rule it is not a peasant, but a bailiff) when he tells you how much milk he gets from his cows, it is horrible! He gets so many gallons of milk a day that anyone knowing the nature of the cow realises it is quite unnatural to get so much milk from a cow. But they manage to get it! Quite certainly gentlemen, they manage to get it! Some of them in my opinion, get up to twice as large a quantity as the cow should really give. In this way the farm can obviously become exceedingly profitable. One cannot even say that it is as yet very noticeable, but the milk has not got the same force as milk produced under normal conditions; one cannot immediately prove the great harm that is being done.

Perhaps I might tell you the following. We have made experiments with a remedy for foot-and-mouth disease in cattle; we have made many such experiments during the last few years. They were carried out on large farms as well as on smaller ones where the milk production was not pushed so far as on the big farms. Much could be learnt in this way because one had to test how the remedy worked in foot-and-mouth disease.

The matter however, was not carried to a conclusion, for the officials in charge did not agree, and today so many concessions and so on, are necessary. But the remedy succeeded well, and with a slight alteration, it has also had very good results in distemper in dogs, under the name of "Distempo."

When one makes these experiments one discovers the following :—

One finds that calves bred from cows that have been brought to an excessive production of milk, are considerably weaker. You see it in the way the remedy affects them. The working or non-working of the remedy, so to speak, can be tremendously increased in such cases. The calf grows up if it does not die of the disease, but the calf bred from a cow that has been over-stimulated to this over-production of milk, a calf of such breeding is weaker than calves bred from cows that have never been so forced. This change can be observed through the first, second, third or fourth generations, but is then so slight that observation is not easy. This breeding for milk-production is still of short standing, but I know very well that if it continues, if a cow is forced to yield six gallons of milk a day, if you continue thus maltreating it, all breeding of cows will after a time go absolutely to ruin. There is nothing to be done.

Well, in artificial bee-keeping things are, naturally not fundamentally so bad, because the bee is a creature that can always help itself again, that is indeed, incredibly able to help itself because the bee lives so much nearer to Nature than the cow that is being bred in this fashion. It is not even quite so bad if cows so maltreated for milk-production are nevertheless at times taken out to pasture. But on the big dairy farms this is no longer done. These farms have nothing but stall-feeding; the cow is completely torn away from natural conditions.

You cannot afford to do this in bee-keeping. Thanks to its nature the bee remains united with external Nature; it helps itself again. And you see, gentlemen, this self-help in the bee-hive is something extremely wonderful.

We now come to what Herr Müller said about the bumble-bees and hornets he sometimes finds in his bee-hives, which did not sting him, whereas it can be sometimes rather a disaster to meet a hornet.

I would like here to tell you something else. I do not know whether those of you who are bee-keepers have already experienced this; it may happen that you have an empty hive, and I once saw a strange thing in an empty hive, something like a lump. At first one could not make out what it was. The bees appeared, apparently for no good reason at all, to have made a lump out of all their usual products, out of all sorts of things. A lump just like a big stone and surrounded by all manner of resin and pitch, glue-like substances, wax and so on; such things as the bees also collect. I was curious to know what this was and I took the lump to pieces, and behold, there was a dead mouse inside!

You see, the mouse had got into the hive and died there, and now imagine what a terrible thing the smell of a dead mouse would have been for the bees! In this emergency the whole colony had the instinct to surround the dead mouse with a shell. When one took this shell to pieces it smelt horribly, but the smell had remained quite shut up within the shell.

You see, gentlemen, within the hive was not only the instinct to build cells, to feed the brood, but, in an emergency, the instinct for something *unusual*, for what has to be done when a dead mouse is in the hive! Since the bees were not sufficient in number to carry the mouse away, they helped themselves; they made a shell all round it.

I have heard from others that snails or slugs which had crept inside hives were also thus encrusted. In the hive not only ordinary instincts are living, but true healing instincts; these are exceedingly active in the hive.

Well—if there is a hornets nest in the hive the bees do not enclose it with a hard shell, but continually surround the nest with excretions of their poison, so that the hornets lose all energy, all power to attack. Just as the mouse, the dead mouse in there can no longer send its smell in all directions, so the hornet, though not so firmly imprisoned, is continually exposed to the exhalations with which the bees surround it, and thereby gets so weakened that they can do nothing. The hornet loses all its strength, and can no longer use its sting to defend itself when you come near it.

It is really so, that one only does justice to the bees when one goes beyond mere intellect and actually follows up the facts with a certain inner vision. It is quite wonderful, this picture. One must therefore say, *the bee-colony is a totality*. It must be seen as a totality. But in a totality the harm does not appear all in a moment.

You see, if one knows men well, one can say for instance, the following:—A man—there are such men—is fairly fresh and strong at the age of 65 or 66; another man is not so fresh because he suffers inwardly from too much lime in his arteries, etc. To observe this, and to bring it into connection with what had occurred in his childhood, is extremely interesting.

For example, one can give a child milk that comes from cows who get too much fodder from a lime-stone soil. Even in the milk with which the child is nourished, the child gets some elements of this limey soil. This may not perhaps be at once evident. A doctor of the kind we have today, may come along and show you a child fed on milk derived from a limey soil, and another child fed with its mother's milk and he says, " It makes no difference at all," and so on. But the child fed on its mother's milk is still fresh at the age of 65 or 66, and the child fed on the cow's milk has too much lime in the blood-vessels at the same age. This is so because man is *a whole*, and what works in one period of time still continues to be active at a much later period. A thing can be entirely healthy at one moment, and yet it works on later.

This is what I mean when I say that from the conditions of bee-keeping today, you cannot draw conclusions as to what artificial methods of bee-keeping signify, or do not signify. One must think how will it be 50, 60 or 100 years hence! It is quite comprehensible that someone should say today—I do not understand how this will be quite different in 50, 60 or 100 years time—this is quite comprehensible.

It once happened to me on a farm, that all in good nature, I was nearly killed when I began to say that one ought not to get so much milk, for the breeding of cows would suffer even sooner, and would be ruined within a quarter of a century. One cannot as yet say very much against these artificial methods in bee-keeping today, because we are now living under conditions in which nothing can be done in the social domain.

But it must be recognised that there is a great difference in whether one allows Nature to take a free course, or whether one brings artificial methods into the matter. I do not want to protest against what Herr Müller has said. It is quite correct. Today one cannot as yet confirm these things; one must wait for this. We will discuss it together in a 100 years time, Herr Müller, and see what your opinion is then! It is a question that cannot be decided at the moment.

(HERR ERBSMHEL once more points out that modern bee-keeping is entirely a matter of making it profitable).

DR. STEINER:

The more you find that a man does his bee-keeping as a hobby, the more you will find him in agreement with the Spaniard whom you quoted just now. This farmer did not do much reckoning up as to profit; this is not generally the case today, but 50 or 60 years ago the farmer did not do much reckoning as to what he could make out of his bees; it was hardly taken into account. He either gave the honey away, or if he sold it, he put the money into the children's money boxes—or something similar. Today, the whole conditions are quite different. One cannot imagine that a man paid by the hour, or in any sense dependent on time for his payment, would not feel himself obliged to take profit-making into account. He is simply driven to it by circumstances. Today there are bee-keepers who as working men, must stay away from their work now and again, must take leave of absence if they want to carry on their bee-keeping in the right way—this is so is it not? (Certainly.) Then, quite naturally, they count up what they did not get—from other work.

Just think for a moment; bee-keeping is so ancient that no one can say today from any external evidence what bee-keeping really was when the bee was still undomesticated. For the most part people know only our bees, I mean the European honey-bees, and they know only domestic bee-keeping. Natural History books write mostly about the bee which is universally spread in Europe, as "the common hive-bee." Thus one only knows about domestic bee-keeping. This is well worth our attention, gentlemen, that one knows only domestic bee-keeping; one is not aware what it was all like when only Nature herself was at work. Bee-keeping is very ancient. And when things are so old as this prices must be fixed on quite a different basis from that on which we mostly work today. For this reason we really have to say that here also we must trust that little by little men will come to realise that better social conditions must be brought about. I believe there will then be less talk as to whether things are profitable or not. These competitive ideas, even if they do not imply competition among those engaged in the production of similar goods, have at any rate to do with those who produce different goods.

I will now answer any other questions connected with what has already been said.

QUESTION:

There are people who cannot digest honey at all. They

immediately get stomach trouble. Is there any way of preventing these bad effects of eating honey?
DR. STEINER:

People who cannot take honey are, as a rule, those who in early life have had some tendency to sclerosis, to a hardening of the whole body, so that the whole digestive process is too slow. That is why they cannot digest honey which tends to accelerate the metabolic process. Because these persons digest too slowly, the honey wants to make it quicker, and so they quarrel with their own digestion, with the result that they have pains in the stomach.

Everybody ought really to be able to enjoy a little honey—that is, not only to "enjoy" it, but to have the inner capacity to do so. When one finds people unable to digest honey, one has first to look for the actual cause. You must not think there is a general remedy, an universal remedy, but one can make use of one remedy or another, dependent on the causes which have resulted in this hardened body. For example, the cause might be as follows: let us say, a man cannot take honey; he gets indigestion. One asks oneself: "Does this man get indigestion because, as we say, he has a tendency to a sclerosis of the head, as it is called, to a calcifying of the veins and arteries, the blood-vessels of the head? It can happen, in this case, that at a certain age he is unable to digest honey. To cure such a man we must take a preparation of phosphorus, and if one can cure him he will then be able to take honey. Or it may also happen that one finds the trouble in the lungs. One must then not take phosphorus, but a preparation of sulphur. Thus the answer to the question is that one cannot say in general that a man has indigestion when he eats honey, how can we cure it? But one must say: "If a man at a certain age is not able to eat honey, it is an illness. A healthy man can eat honey. If he cannot digest it he is ill, and one must find out what is wrong with him and cure it. Not to be able to digest honey is, however, less important than not to be able to take sugar, as, for instance, when a man has "*diabetes mellitus*," or sugar-sickness. This, of course, is worse, then he is really ill, much more so than when he cannot digest honey. But even in this case he is somewhat ill and one must cure the illness.

QUESTION:

Like most other insects, in the dark, bees will fly towards candle or lamp-light. I have been frequently assured by experienced bee-keepers that bees are much less attracted by electric light. When one goes to them with a pocket electric torch they keep quite quiet, as though they did not notice the light at all. Only after some little time do they get restless Lamp or candle-light affects them much more quickly, and in greater numbers. Is there any explanation for this behaviour? Herr Müller says he has observed the same thing.

DR. STEINER:

You will probably have seen, gentlemen, in the old Goetheanum, that the cupolas were painted inside with different colours, colours made from pure vegetable substances. But this making of colours from various plant-substances finally proved that they would have completely faded away if the Sun had shone into the cupola. If one had exposed these colours for some little time, they might have lasted perhaps for some months, perhaps a few years, but exposed to direct sunlight they would have faded so much one would have seen nothing more of the paintings once there.

But exposed to the electric light, they remained. We therefore, used these colours in a way that a painter working in sunlight could not have done at all. In the sunlight they would have faded completely away, whereas in electric light they were permanent.

So you see, sunlight which has chemical properties (and you said bees were aware of this) has effects quite different to those of electric light. Electric light works on all substances in a much more hardening way, it does not dissolve them. That is why the bees feel something like a very slight cramp which they do not feel with sunlight, though of course, they recover again.

QUESTION:

With regard to the influences of the Signs of the Zodiac on honey production, the peasants lay great stress on sowing seed when the moon is in the sign of the Twins, and so on. The question is whether this idea as to the Signs of the Zodiac is founded on external data, or if there is more than this in it?

DR STEINER:

You see, gentlemen, today these things are never dealt with scientifically. But one can treat them scientifically. On the whole colony of bees, as such, there is as I told you, an influence. The bee, and above all the Queen is, in a certain sense, a Sun creature, and thus all that the Sun experiences in that it passes through the Zodiac, has the greater influence. But the bees naturally, depend on the plants, and here indeed, the sowing, the scattering of the seed, can be very much affected by the passage of the moon through a zodiacal sign; this concerns the preparatory substances the bees are able to find in the plants.

These things are by no means fanciful, but as a rule they are represented quite superficially; they should be much more deeply studied.

We have now come to the end of our time. What has to be said further we will discuss next Saturday at 9 o'clock. I think many of you have questions at heart. Bee-keeping is so beautiful and of such great value that one cannot ask enough about it. Ask questions of one another, of Herr Müller, and of me. I believe we shall find a balancing of our contradictory opinions. We need not get our stings ready like the bees but can peacefully discuss them all. But questions must be asked honestly and without reserve.

LECTURE VI.
Dornach, December 10, 1923.

HERR DOLLINGER wishes to ask a question about the honeycomb. There are people who eat the wax as well as the honey, and in restaurants they used at times to serve honey in the comb. He would like to know if it was a bad thing to eat the comb.

As to the diseases of bees, he thinks these could not formerly have been as bad as they are today when the bees are overexploited.

HERR MUELLER said that eating comb-honey was an idiosyncrasy with some people. Naturally, these are the natural combs and not artificial ones. He does not think that bee diseases are the result of exploitation, but that formerly they were less considered. In those days there were not so many weak stocks and so one was not so much on the look out for them. A disease had appeared in Switzerland from England which had not been known in the past. Herr Erbsmehl thinks this may perhaps be owing to the use of artificial manures, even the flowers sicken as the result of this.

DR. STEINER:

With regard to these two points, one might say it is quite true that the eating of honey-comb is a fancy with some people; the real question is whether it is good for them, and this can, unfortunately only be answered medically. It is only possible to answer this question when one is really able to observe these people who eat the honey-comb, thus the wax, from the point of view of their state of health. I have seen various people who eat the comb, but they always spat it out when they had sucked out the honey. I have not so far come across people who eat any considerable quantity of wax. One should take into consideration that people digest in very different ways, not everyone in the same way. There may be people who would get some kind of gastric trouble simply by eating the wax, and such persons should be advised not to take it. But there can also be people who are able to digest the wax without any trouble and get rid of the residue by excretion. With regard to these people one could certainly say that because they eat the wax *with* the honey, (thus leaving the honey as long as possible still in connection with the wax which has entered the body), the honey is digested more in the intestines, whereas *otherwise* it is not digested till it has left the intestines and has passed into the lymphatic vessels. It is a question of the state of health of the person concerned. There are people who digest more in the intestines, and others more in the lymphatic vessels; one cannot say that one way is better than the other, for one is just as good as the other. It depends on the individual. One could only speak with certainty if one took a number of people who eat honey in the comb, and others who eat it without the comb, and then investigated how these two matters are related.

With regard to bee-diseases the question is, as is usual in disease, namely, that we must take into account what Herr Müller has just said. It is so even with human beings that certain things were not much noticed formerly, whereas today they are most carefully studied. But here something essentially different comes in question. The bee-keeper of the past had really many good instincts: he did many things without being able to say just why he did them. Today these instincts no longer exist. Today people always want to know the reason why. To determine this *why* it is, however, necessary to study the whole matter very fundamentally. Modern knowledge is not as a rule in a position to do this.

You see, the bee-keeper of old had very good instincts as how to treat the bees, I should like to say, in quite a personal manner. For instance, you should consider that there is already a considerable difference between giving the bees the old straw skeps as in former days, and giving them wooden hives as one does today. Box-hives are made of wood, and wood is an entirely different substance to the straw of which the old skeps were made. Straw attracts quite other substances from the air than does wood, so we have already a difference in the external handling. When I add to this all the bee-keeper did in former times, and above all, the strong instincts he had to do them even if he did not always know the reason why, he would, for example, place his bee-hives on some chosen spot, where the wind would blow more often from one quarter or another, and so on. Today one sets the bee-hives wherever there is room for them, from reasons of convenience. The climatic elements are still considered, but no longer to the same degree.

HERR MUELLER stated that he pays great attention to this; he places his hives on a ridge where they are sheltered from the north wind and the east wind, and so on.

DR. STEINER:

In such matters wood is less sensitive than straw. I have no intention of agitating in favour of straw skeps; nevertheless differences do exist, and just such things as these certainly, very definitely, affect the bees with regard to their inner activities. A tremendous activity goes on in the body of the bee when it must first gather the nectar from the plants, and in absorbing it, transforms it. This is really an immense work. How does the bee accomplish it? It is accomplished through the quite special relationship between the two different fluids in the bee. One of these is the gastric juices and the other the blood-fluid. When you study the bee you find the whitish gastric juice and the reddish sap of the blood; these are the two main elements of which the bee is constituted, and all the other parts are arranged according to the workings of the gastric juice and the blood.

The main point then is this definite proportion between these two fluids; they differ very considerably in themselves. The gastric juice is what one calls acid in chemistry, and the blood sap is chemically called alkaline, which means that it is not acid though it can be made so; in itself it is however, not acid. When the pepsin is insufficiently acid, something takes place within the bee which greatly disturbs its inner organism in the honey-producing process. The blood sap is only kept sufficiently strong when the necessary climatic conditions of light and warmth, etc., are present.

It will therefore be very important to take the right means of establishing the proper balance between the gastric fluid and the blood if one is to overcome the many diseases which have recently appeared among the bees. As bee-keeping can no longer be carried on as in past days, it is no longer possible to arrive at preventive methods through climatic conditions of warmth, etc., for these are no longer able to work so effectively upon the stocks of bees today; one will have to discover what will be able to work most favourably on the blood sap of the bee. It will be necessary in the future that bee-keepers take special care that the blood sap of the bee is rightly provided for. The following is important: you all know that there are years when the bees are obliged to get nectar almost exclusively from trees. In such seasons the composition of the blood sap is endangered, and the bees are much more liable to disease than at other times. It will be necessary in the future that the bee-keeper even contrives a small green-house—it need not be a large one—in which he can cultivate those plants which the bees not only like, but must have at certain times of the year. It will be necessary to have at least some small plot of flowers for the bees especially, for instance in the month of May. They will not fail to discover them for themselves whenever the plants they need have failed elsewhere. By this special cultivation of the necessary plants in the neighbourhood of the hives it will be possible to combat these diseases. These are methods I can recommend; I am giving only indications, but they will most certainly prove satisfactory for they are derived from a knowledge of bee-keeping. If they are put to the test you will find that one day they will bear very good fruit for the bee-keeper, for he will find that the diseases of bees can be prevented by these means. But if one is to proceed in a practical way all the connections mentioned above must be taken into account. I have no wish to make assertions; I only wish to say that these things arise out of the whole nature of the bees, and that it would be well to make experiments with especially cultivated plants in seasons when those most needed have failed, either partially or altogether. It should be possible in this way to considerably improve the health of the bees. I am myself quite convinced that these methods will prove successful when one is able to enter once again into these questions with a true understanding of nature. You see, it is not possible to go back to the old methods of bee-keeping. Just as little as there is any need to be reactionary in the realms of politics, or of life, is there any necessity to be a reactionary in any other domain. One must move with the times; but what really matters is that while we leave the old methods we are careful to balance this by something which will replace what we have lost. This is essential.

HERR MUELLER stated that bee-keepers were already working in the direction of the special cultivation of certain plants. For example, the yellow crocus, which is grown in large quantities for the bees; other plants were cultivated also with similar small yellow blossoms. Indeed, more than this, for a large amount of American clover is now planted; a clover which grows six feet in height and flowers the whole year round. It is cut only in the autumn; till then the blossom is left for the bees. This might also be necessary perhaps?

DR. STEINER:

Certainly, such things are no doubt done, but as a rule the right connections are not known. What Herr Müller had mentioned at first, was excellent and should be continued, but with regard to the American clover that flowers all the year round, this will in future be avoided, for this plant cannot bring about any improvement at all in the blood-sap of the bees; it acts only as a stimulant, and for a very short time. It is very much the same as trying to cure a man with alcohol, the bees are stimulated to more activity for a certain time. The very greatest care should really be taken today not to grow plants for the bees that are totally foreign to them; bees in their whole organic nature are bound up with a particular country. This is very evident, for the bees from different parts of the world differ widely from one another. There is, for instance, the mid-European bee already referred to here, the common domestic bee. The Italian bee again is quite unlike the Spanish bee, and so on. Bees are most strongly bound by their habits to their native country, and one cannot help them in any real way by giving them the nectar or honey belonging to entirely different countries. They have then, so much work to do in their own bodies that there are great disturbances there; the bees are forced to try and adapt themselves, to make their organisation as much as possible like that of the bees over there, in those countries where the clover comes from. Hard facts will prove in time that though such methods may appear successful for a few years, disastrous results will follow. It is quite true as has been said, that so far there are no definite indications of this, but it will none the less occur, and then people must abandon all such methods, or continue them as was done in the case of the vines. You will remember that in the seventies or eighties, phyloxera appeared and is destroying the vineyards of Europe, over immense areas. At the time I was able to study this matter, as I had a very good friend who was a farmer, and who also edited an agricultural paper, and gave much attention to this whole problem. People began to wonder why the American vine appeared immune to this disease. But what did it all amount to? It amounted to this, that the remedies by which the disease could be got rid of with the American vine, could not be used with the same result on the

European vine. The consequence was, that even when everyone began to cultivate the American vine, they could succeed in keeping it in health, whereas the European vines died out. The cultivation of the European vine had to be given up altogether; the whole cultivation of the vineyards was Americanised, and everything has been completely changed. This has happened in many places. To think in this mechanical manner is valueless; one must be quite clear that things through their whole nature may be bound up with definite localities, and this fact must be taken into account. Otherwise though some temporary success may follow, it cannot be permanent.

Are there any other questions you would like to ask? Or are all you gentlemen content to eat honey without so much discussion about it? Perhaps some question may occur to one or another of you.

Meanwhile, I should like to say something quite briefly about the nature of this honey-making process of the bees. It is something so really wonderful that there should be these tiny little creatures that are able to transform what they have gathered from the flowers or plants in general, into the honey which is so health-giving, and which should really play a far greater part in the nourishment of men and women today. It is not realised how important the consumption of honey actually is. For example, if it were possible to influence the social medicine of today, it would be discovered that if people about to be married would eat honey as a preparation for the future, they would not have ricketty children. Honey when assimilated can affect the reproductive processes, and greatly influence the building up of the body of the child. The consumption of honey by the parents, and above all by the prospective mother, works especially into the bony structure of the child. Results such as this will appear when these questions are considered in their essential aspects. In the place of the trivialities put forward in scientific journals today, it will be asked, when once we have some real knowledge of these things: "What is it best to eat at this or that time of life?" "What is best at another time of life?" Indeed, gentlemen, this will be of immense value, for the general state of health will then essentially improve, and more especially will this affect a man's vitality. Today people attach very little value to such matters. Those whose children do not suffer from rickets are naturally very pleased, but they do not think very much about it, it is taken as a matter of course. Only those complain whose children are born with rickets. It is just in the case of such most valuable social and medical methods that people remain indifferent, for it is generally taken for granted that such measures are concerned merely with what they regard as a normal condition. They have first to be persuaded that this is not the case. It should, however, be recognised that extremely favourable results would appear in this direction, and I am sure that if it could in this way be realised that through spiritual science it is possible to arrive at such conclusions, people would begin to look towards the things of the spirit. They would do this to a far greater extent than at present, when they are only told to pray that this or that may happen. Truly, gentlemen, these things which can be learnt by the spirit, and which modern science ignores, are such that one is able to know that during the times of betrothal and pregnancy, honey can be of inestimable value.

I have just said that it is a most wonderful thing that the bee should be able to gather substances from the storehouse of nature and then transform them into this honey which is of so great value to human life. You will best understand on what the origin of honey actually rests if I describe to you the same process in the quite different form in which it appears in those relatives of the bees, if I may call them so, the wasps.

The wasps do not provide man with honey, but they prepare a substance that can be made use of medicinally, though of a very different kind to that prepared for us by the bees. In the next lecture I will also speak about the ants, but first will we consider a certain species of wasp. There are wasps that have the peculiarity that they do not deposit their eggs at random, but place them on plants or on the leaves or bark of trees, even into the blossoms of trees.* Here for example is the branch, here an oak-leaf, and the wasp with its ovipositor which is hollow, (the sting would be here) lays its egg in the oak-leaf, or in some other part of a plant. What then happens? Where the egg has been placed the whole surrounding tissue of the leaf is changed; the leaf would have been quite different if the egg had not been laid there. Very good, let us now see what has happened.

The whole growth of the plant has been affected, and protruding from the leaf, entirely surrounding the little wasp-egg, we find the so-called gall-nut or gall-apple, those little brownish coloured nuts or apples so often seen on trees. They are there because a wasp deposited an egg at this spot, and all round the egg there is this metamorphosed plant-substance which entirely envelops it. The wasp egg would perish if it were laid in any other place; it can only exist and develop because this protective substance encloses it which the gall-wasp steals from the plant. The wasp robs the plant of this substance. You see, the bee lays its egg in the cells of the comb; the larvæ develop and emerge as bees, which in their turn steal the substance of the plant, and elaborate it within themselves. The wasp does this at an earlier stage, for in the depositing of the egg the wasp already takes from the plant the substance it needs. The bee, as it were, waits a little longer, the wasp does it earlier. In the case of the higher animals, and with man, the egg is already surrounded with a protecting sheath within the body of the mother. In this instance what the wasp has to take from the plant is provided by the mother. This gall-nut is simply built up from the substance of the plant, just as the chorion is formed as a sheath round the egg in the body of the mother, and is ejected later with the after-birth.

---

*Drawing on the blackboard.

You see how close is the relationship between the wasp and the plant. In districts especially rich in wasps one can find trees almost entirely covered with these galls. The wasp lives with the trees; it depends on them, for its eggs would never develop if it could not procure this protective covering from the different trees or plants. These galls have very many and various forms, there are some which do not look like small apples, but are interwoven and hairy, but everywhere the small germ of the wasp is in the centre. At times these galls look like shaggy little nuts. We see how close is the relationship between the wasps and the plants with which they share their existence.

When the wasp has matured, it eats its way with its sharp jaws out of the gall-nut, and emerges as a wasp, and after a period of living in the outer world lays its eggs on a leaf or the bark of a tree; the egg and larval stages are always passed through as a living together with the plants.

Well, gentlemen, you may perhaps say—what has all this to do with the production of honey? It has actually a great deal to do with it, for when such things are observed in the right way one learns to know how the honey was first prepared in nature, and we find once more an instance of how the instinctive knowledge of the people in older times took these things into account.

Perhaps some of you know that in the south, and more especially in Greece, the cultivation of fig trees is of much importance. These are the so-called wild figs which are certainly rather sweet, but there are people with a still sweeter tooth, who wish to have fig trees that bore still sweeter figs than those of the wild trees. What do these people do?

Now just imagine you have a wild fig tree; this wild fig tree is a special favourite with a certain kind of wasp which lays its eggs upon it. Let us picture this tree, and on its branches a wild fig into which the wasp inserts its egg. Now the grower of the figs is in his way a clever fellow; he lets the wasps lay their eggs in the wild figs which he cultivates just for this very purpose. Later this fellow gathers two of these figs, just at the moment when the wasp eggs are not quite fully developed, when the wasps are not yet ready to creep out, and he takes a reed and ties the two figs together so that they are held firmly. And now he goes to a fig tree that he wants to improve, and he hangs the two figs he has tied together, and within which are the eggs of the wasp not yet fully developed, and binds them on to the fig-tree which he wishes to sweeten. And now the following happens: the wasps within the figs feel that something has happened, for the figs which were gathered now begin to dry up, for they are no longer supplied with the sap of the tree, and get very dry. The immature wasp inside senses this, even the egg is aware of it, and the result is that the wasp is in a terrible hurry to come out of the fig. The grower always starts this process in the spring; he first lets the wasp lay its eggs, and in the month of May he quickly gathers the two figs and carries out his plan. The little creature inside thinks, now I must hurry up, now the time has come when the figs dry up. In a terrible hurry the wasp emerges much earlier than it would otherwise have done. If the fig had remained where it was before, it would only have crept out in the late summer; now it must creep out in the early summer with the result that there is a second brood. It lays eggs in the summer which would otherwise have been laid in the following spring. Now these late eggs which are deposited on the tree that is to be further cultivated, do not reach full maturity, they only develop to a certain stage. The result of this is, that those figs into which the second brood has been placed become twice as sweet as the wild figs. This is the method of improving the figs, of making them twice as sweet.

What has actually happened here? The wasps, which though they differ from the bees are yet related to them, the wasps take just that substance from the plant which is on the way to become honey. If in the clever way of the cultivator of the fig trees, the figs of the wild tree containing the eggs of the wasp are thrown up and tied so that they remain hanging up there, and if one then is clever enough to induce the wasps to weave again into the tree what they have taken from the other tree, then honey in the form of sweetness is, as it were, filtered into these grafted fig-trees; it enters into the figs in the form of sweetness because the wasps have prepared it in an extremely fine state of dilution; Nature itself has brought it about in an indirect way.

You see, gentlemen, nothing has been taken away from Nature, the essence of the honey remains within Nature. The wasp cannot prepare the honey in the way the bee does, for its organisation is not adapted to this. But when, by this by-path, it is compelled during the stages of its growth, to carry the sweetness of the honey from one fig-tree to another, the sweetness of the grafted figs can be increased; a kind of honey-substance is then within them.

You see, gentlemen, we arrive here at something very interesting. It seems that these wasps have a body which is unable to gather the nectar, the honey-substance from Nature, and transform it into honey within itself. But man can bring it about that from one fig-tree to another a kind of honey-making takes place. The bee is therefore a creature that develops a wasp-like body so much further that it is able to accomplish this quite apart from the trees; in the case of the wasp the process must be left within the tree itself. So we must say: the bee retains within itself more of that force which the wasp only possesses at a very young stage, as long, that is, as it is in the egg, or larval state. When the wasp develops further it loses the power of producing honey; the bee retains it and can make use of it as a fully matured creature.

Just think, gentlemen, what it signifies that one can in this way look into Nature's processes, and can say to oneself: within the plants there is concealed this honey, this substance that tends towards sugar-sweetness. It is there; it shows itself, if only one follows the right path; one has only to assist Nature by seeing that the wasp comes at the right moment to the tree that is to be improved.

Here, in our country such things cannot be done, it is no longer possible today. There was once a time in the evolution of the earth when from the wasps, which as long as 2,000 years ago, and indeed, still today, could be persuaded by some clever fellow to produce a second brood as I have described. These wasps crept out and were given the opportunity of laying their eggs in the figs, which were then again and again gathered. Thus, in the course of time, it was possible that bees could be developed from these wasps.

The bee is a creature which in very ancient times was developed from the wasp. Today one can still see that is by means of an *animal activity*, namely that of the wasps, that honey is first prepared in the realms of nature.

So now, you can also understand how closely related to this is the fact that the bees place their honey in the cells of the honey-comb. This comb consists mainly of wax, and wax is not only necessary in order that the bees may deposit their honey there, for the bee can only produce honey when its whole organism is active in the right way. It must therefore secrete wax.

The second fig tree in which sweetness arises of itself, is also richer in wax than the wild tree. It differs especially from the wild tree in that it is richer in wax. Nature has herself increased the wax so that the cultivated figs, the sweetened figs, grow on a tree which in a certain way, Nature has made richer in wax.

You can already see here a model, as it were, for what appears in bee-keeping.

If you now go to work very carefully, and make a cross-section from the trunk of the cultivated fig tree, you will find, if you look carefully, patterns just like the wax cells of the comb. Within the tree-trunk you find certain growths similar to the honey cells, formed from the precipitated wax of the tree. The tree that is richer in wax uses it in a kind of honey-cell formation.

So we can say: when we study this special cultivation of the fig trees we discover a kind of honey production in Nature that has not yet appeared openly, for the honey remains within the figs. The bees, if I may so express it, bring out into the open what remains still within Nature in the sweetened figs. Thus, what would otherwise have remained within the tree-trunk, forming there these natural cells, which are only less definite, less substantial than the bee cells, and fade away again, this whole wax and honey-making process is driven up into the figs, so that Nature is herself a bee-keeper. The bees have drawn it forth from Nature and have these processes within themselves.

What does the bee then do? The bee deposits its eggs within the hive, and the egg matures there. It does not need to change the substance into a gall-apple, it takes the nectar directly from the plants, neither does the bee need to go to the tree that is richer in wax, for she accomplishes in herself what takes place in the tree-trunk, and deposits in the comb the juices of the plant which she transforms into honey, which in the case of the cultivated tree, remains in the juices of the fig. One can say that what in Nature lies concealed in the tree through the wasps, now happens outwardly, and it becomes clear what it really is that we have before us, when we look into the hive with its marvellously built comb of waxen cells. It is indeed, gentlemen, a wonderful sight, is it not Herr Müller? A wonderful sight is the artistic construction of these waxen cells with the honey within them.

You have only to look at it gentlemen, and you will say to yourselves—the bees with their waxen combs really show us a kind of artistically formed tree-trunk with its many branches. The bee does not need to go to the tree to lay her eggs there, but they build for themselves a kind of picture of a tree, and in the place of the figs growing there, she puts honey into the finished cells. We find, as it were, a copy of the artificially cultivated fig tree which the bees have made.

Truly, gentlemen, this is to look into the very heart of Nature, and realise what can be learnt from her. Men have yet to learn much from Nature, but for this they must first learn to recognise the spiritual in Nature. Without this recognition of the spirit in Nature, one merely stands and gapes, and should one journey to the south and see how those clever fellows there tie the figs together, the figs pierced by the wasps, and throw them up into the trees and bind and fix them there we shall gape as tourists do, even when they are scientific gentlemen, and not know what to make of it, They do not know that he saves the bees their labour, for Nature will put the honey into the figs for him.

In those countries where figs are plentiful, they are as health-giving as honey, for it is honey at an earlier stage of development that is already in the figs.

You see, these are things which we ought to know if we are to discuss a matter of such importance as bee-keeping. I believe that by such means we shall in time arrive at points of view of true value.

LECTURE VII.

Dornach, December 12, 1923.

(Questions were asked as to the affinity between bees and flowers which unites them so closely; also, what honey should be, and is, in relation to man.

The question of the laying of eggs when the Queen is not fecundated was again raised, as in a normal hive there are three kinds of eggs: queen-eggs, worker-eggs and drone-eggs).

DR. STEINER:
Very well, we will discuss these things once more in today's lecture. It is like this: we have first the fertilisation of the Queen during the nuptial flight. The Queen is then fecundated. Then we have to consider the time which elapses between the laying of the eggs until the insect is completely matured, till the bee is there. With the Queen this period is sixteen days, with the worker-bee twenty-one—twenty-two days, and in the case of the drone twenty-two—twenty-four days. We have then to begin with these three types; they differ from one another in so far as they mature during differing periods of time. What lies at the root of this? When a bee develops as a Queen it is due to the special feeding it has been given; the Queen larvæ are differently fed so that growth is accelerated. Now the bees are creatures of the Sun, and the Sun needs approximately the same time to revolve once upon its own axis as the worker-bee needs to come to maturity. The Queen does not wait in her development till the Sun has quite completed this revolution, and for this reason her whole development remains entirely within the influence of the Sun. Thereby she becomes a creature capable of laying eggs; all that is connected with a capacity to lay eggs is under the influence of the Sun, and indeed, of the whole cosmos also. The moment the feeding is such that development proceeds at the rate of the worker-bee, which is that of almost a complete revolution of the Sun, the nearer the bee approaches the influence of the earth-evolution. The farther the Sun moves, the more the bee comes under the influences of the earth. The worker-bee is indeed largely a creature of the Sun, but already somewhat of an earthly creature. But the drone which develops during a longer period than is necessary for a complete revolution of the Sun, becomes a creature wholly of the earth. It withdraws itself from the influence of the Sun.

We have then this trinity; we have the Queen, the worker-bees, in which there are still super-earthly forces, and we have the drones which have no longer anything to do with the Sun, but are fully creatures of the earth. All else that happens occurs no longer under the influence of the earth, with the one exception of the actual fecundation of the Queen.

Now this is the remarkable point. Just consider this nuptial flight of the Queen. The lower animals dislike fecundation, they seek to avoid it. This is everywhere in evidence. Thus the flight of the Queen is an escape towards the Sun, and no fecundation can take place when the day is dull. The drones who try to bring an earthly element into the Sun element must even wrestle in the air, and the weaker ones are left behind. Only the very strongest can fly as high as the Queen, and fertilise her. But even after this has taken place it is not all the eggs that are fertilised, but only a portion of them, and these can become Queens or worker-bees; the remaining portion that are unfertilised within the body of the Queen become drones. When the Queen is not fecundated then only drones can emerge, when she is fecundated, Queens, worker-bees and drones can emerge, because the seed is fertilised and the heavenly has made contact with the earthly. Thus even when there are worker-bees and drones, the latter still owe their origin to a longer exposure to earthly influences, because no fertilisation has in their case taken place, and they must therefore be all the more exposed to earthly influences if they are to become fitted for life; they must be fed for a longer period of time.

QUESTION:

Some years ago, I was told that if anyone has rheumatism and gets stung by a bee or a wasp, the rheumatism will get better.

DR. STEINER:

This touches upon a question which was perhaps not fully considered last Monday. Herr Müller then told us of a man who evidently had some slight affection of the heart, and who collapsed on being stung by a bee.

HERR MUELLER:

The doctor advised him to give up bee-keeping, as otherwise it might be the death of him.

DR. STEINER:

Disease of the heart is a sign that the ego-organisation is not functioning rightly. You have already heard something of these things in former lectures. You will remember that we distinguished four different parts of a man; first of all, the ordinary physical body, which we can touch, secondly the etheric body, thirdly the astral body, and fourthly the ego-organisation.

This ego-organisation is active in the blood; actually, it brings the blood into movement, and in accordance with the movement of the blood, the heart beats. In text books you will always find the facts quite falsely stated, for it is represented as though the heart were a kind of pump, and that this pumping of the heart sends the blood all over the body. This is nonsense, because it is in reality the blood which is brought into motion by the ego-organisation, and moves throughout the body. If anyone asserts that it is the heart that drives the blood, then he must equally assert that if he has a turbine, it is the turbine that sets the water in motion, though everyone knows that it is the water that drives the turbine. Man has the same kind of points of resistance in his heart; the blood comes up against them and sets the heart in motion; thus it is that the ego-organisation works directly in the circulation of the blood.

Now it is actually the case that this ego-organisation is in a mysterious way present in the poison of the bee; it is a similar force to the force that circulates in your blood that is present in the bee-poison. It is of great interest that the bee should have need of this poison within her. The bee does not merely need it in order to be able to sting; that is merely incidental. The bee needs the poison throughout its whole organism, for it must have the same force of circulation that man has in his blood.

The colony of bees, as I told you, is like an entire man. Now consider, you get some of this bee-poison into your body, that is, into your blood, for any poison entering the body goes immediately into the blood. You are, let us say, a normal man, your blood will come more into motion, and inflammation may follow, but your heart can bear it. If however, a man has some disease of the heart, and his ego-organisation is made stronger by the poison, then this affects the weak heart, and the result may be that the man faints, or may even die. This explains the case mentioned by Herr Müller.

The remarkable thing is this; that substances that can make a man ill or even kill him, can also cure him. This is one of the great responsibilities one has in the preparation of medicines, for there are no real remedies which, if wrongly applied, cannot cause the same illnesses which they can also cure.

What then actually happens when a fainting fit or even death results from the sting of a bee?

You see, when a man faints, then his astral body, and more especially his ego-organisation, has withdrawn from the body as happens in sleep, only in sleep this happens in a normal way, and in a swoon in abnormal way. In a swoon, or fainting fit, the astral body does not withdraw completely as in sleep, it gets stuck fast, and when a man has a weak ego-organisation, he cannot bring it back again. One has to shake him, wake him up, rouse him out of his faintness by making him breathe more strongly by certain movements. You know how in these cases, one has to take the man's arms, cross them over on his breast, put them back, then again bring them forward and so on, and this artificial breathing really always means that one is trying to bring the ego-organisation back into the body in the right way.

And now let us suppose someone is suffering from rheumatism, or perhaps gout, or other deposits in the body; then one must try to strengthen the ego-organisation. Why do people have gout or rheumatism? Because the ego-organisation is too weak and cannot bring the blood into the right movement. The blood must be made to move more quickly. When the blood is not in the right state, when for instance, it flows too slowly, minute crystals are precipitated everywhere, and pass into the neighbourhood of the blood-vessels. These minute crystals consist of uric acid, and they go all over the body, and cause gout or rheumatism—the ego-organisation is too weak.

If I now give this man the right dose of bee or wasp poison, his ego-organisation is strengthened; only one must not give too much, or the ego-organisation might not be able to hold its own. But if one gives just enough to strengthen the ego one can then find a very good remedy prepared from the bee or wasp poison; only one must combine it with some other substance. These things are done. For instance, the old Tartarus remedy is manufactured in a similar way, though from different substances.

Remedies can always be prepared from poisonous substances, as in this case for the strengthening of the ego-organisation, but in applying them it is necessary to know all about the particular patient. For example, someone has gout or rheumatism; the first question must be—is his heart sound? that is, does it function well under the influence of the blood-circulation? If this is the case, he can be cured with bee or wasp poison. If the heart is not sound (but here one must distinguish between a nervous heart trouble, where it is less harmful) but if you have a patient with a serious heart disease, when the trouble is due to a valvular disease, then one must be very careful in the use of this remedy. Bee or wasp poison acts very powerfully on the cardiac valve, and when this is diseased these remedies cannot sometimes be made use of at all. This is why it is so dangerous to speak in a general way of some medicine or another as a cure for this or that illness. But one is entitled to say—I make a certain preparation, a remedy; I put wasp or bee poison into it (we actually have such a remedy) combining it with some binding substance, some gelatinous or other vegetable binding substance, which is then put into an *ampoule* and injected, just as the sting of the bee is injected, only the re-action from the bee sting is much stronger. One can prepare this remedy, and can call it a cure for rheumatism.

But even so, this is not the only anxiety one has, for one has first of all to discover whether the patient's general state of health can well bear the remedy; medicaments which enter deeply into the body must only be given when one has most thoroughly examined the patient's whole state of health. For this reason such remedies as enter deeply into the body must only be administered when one has thoroughly examined the patient's state of health.

When one hears of all manner of remedies such as are commonly advertised as cures for one thing or another, they are usually more or less harmless, and may be of use. There are many of these remedies to be bought, and one may agree that this is so, even when they have unpleasant results. Cures very frequently have unpleasant consequences, and the patient usually has to recover from the remedy which has cured him!

If we have some fine strong fellow who has rheumatism, it is as a rule, not true rheumatism, but a gouty condition, and then, as Mr. Burle said, " a few bee-stings can affect him very favourably." He can be cured because he is able to stand the reaction. It is usually so, that a normal man who suffers from rheumatism, and is given the correct dose of bee-poison, can take this remedy well and be cured by it. On the other hand, a bee-sting may cause such severe inflammation that this must first be reduced and the poison, as far as possible, removed, in which case not very much will remain for curing the rheumatism. In the case of a normal man, it will very probably happen that not sufficient will remain over to cure the rheumatism.

But now let us consider the following case. Rheumatism can also come about in this way. A man is perhaps not a very hard worker, and has a very good appetite. Well, generally speaking, a man will have quite a good sound heart if he does not work too much and eats heartily, until the whole situation begins to be rather doubtful.

The heart is an organ with extraordinary powers of resistance, it can hardly be seriously damaged unless there is some hereditary tendency, or if it has been injured in youth; the heart can only be injured after many years. But a man who is a heavy eater often takes a good deal of alcohol with his meals, then the ego-organisation is over-stimulated, and the circulation of the blood becomes too violent; the heart can no longer keep pace with its beats. Poison, uric acid, is deposited all over him; the heart may still be strong for quite a long time, but already gout and rheumatism are lurking everywhere. Under these conditions, a bee-sting may render him extraordinarily good service.

HERR BURLE:

I do not know whether there was a trace of alcoholism about this man I mentioned.

DR. STEINER:

You mean you made no inquiries? You see, gentlemen, when one has such remedies as bee-poison, which is a very powerful one, then one must be quite sure that most careful attention is given to the patient's whole state of health.

HERR MUELLER stated that he got an attack of rheumatism by catching cold; he treated it with exposure to the Sun, after which it disappeared. This summer he had it again slightly. He also believed that one could be cured by bee-stings, but one unlucky day he was badly stung on both legs, and had about thirty-two stings. The only ill effect was that for a week he was all colours of the rainbow. Swelling did not always follow; human bodies are very differently constituted. As already stated, one man may die of a bee-sting, while another may get as many as sixty without his heart beating any faster for it. One man has more resistance than another.

DR. STEINER:

When you got so many stings, was it after you had been working many years with bees?

HERR MUELLER:

Many years.

DR. STEINER:

Probably you no longer remember the first time you were stung. After the first time one gets to feel it either more, or less. The man of whom you told us, was no doubt, stung for the first time. When one has once had a poison in one's body, that is, in the blood, one gets more and more able to cope with it, one gets increasingly immune, as it is called. When someone is stung a bit at the beginning of his bee-keeping, and is otherwise a man with a healthy heart, then the poison so works on him that he becomes less and less sensitive to it. If one knows one is strong and healthy, one can even let oneself be stung once or twice in order that one can be stung afterwards. Rainbow colours show that the poison only affects the skin; the blood has become immune. This does not depend only on the organisation, but on what has been previously introduced into the blood. I am surprised that the doctor who saw this man of whom you told us, did not tell him that the second time it would not be so bad, and the third time he would be immune. But perhaps his heart was so bad he could not safely have taken this risk. That also has to be considered.

And indeed today it is a dangerous affair, because the doctors having once got hold of such things, now think that every bee-master should be inoculated before he starts bee-keeping.

When men go to war they are inoculated with all sorts of poisons, a thing not at all to be recommended, for the blood is then very greatly injured. The blood always deteriorates somewhat when such things are put into it. After a time it recovers its balance, the blood becomes healthy again, but is protected against any fresh poison of the same nature.

HERR MUELLER:

About the drones and the different kinds of eggs, Dr. Steiner has said so much, but one point is perhaps not familiar to him. When one has reason to believe the colony to be healthy, there may be times when the Queen is inferior, or is too old, and all the eggs she lays turn out drones. After many years of experience he is convinced that the Queen, when not a good one or too old, is still capable of laying eggs, some of which are good, but the majority will produce only drones.

Then about honey; how the bee actually makes the honey, and whether the bee-keeper should not help by sugar-feeding. From what had been said here, it would seem that the bee-keeper is on no account to use sugar; it seems that anyone who feeds his bees with sugar will get his name on the black list. It is true that one can have bad experiences with feeding foreign honey.

DR. STEINER:

Naturally, it is quite right to say that one does not get the same product if sugar is fed artificially. If anyone likes taking sugar with honey he can add some for himself. Just as one does not water the wine you offer people on the ground that people should not drink it so strong, one offers what is printed on the label. The best thing in regard to honey is reciprocal control by the bee-keepers, because they best understand the whole question.

With regard to the drones, I should like to say this. One may certainly suspect that the Queen is not properly fertilised; too many drones come out. If one does not wish to leave the matter to the bees to settle, something can be done by means of special feeding, (these experiments have been made) the brood then emerges earlier, *i.e.*, after twenty—twenty-two days, instead of twenty-three—twenty-four days, The drones then appear as somewhat drowsy, but still approximately similar to worker bees. One cannot certainly continue this for long; it is merely an example of the effects of the time-periods.

Such things are however, not done in practical bee-keeping; theoretically, it can certainly be stated that a very great deal depends on the feeding, and it is undeniable that an irregularly egg-laying bee can be developed from a worker-bee, though it will certainly not be a real Queen. These things all go to show how readily transformable these creatures are, but such matters have no great value in practical bee-keeping.

HERR MUELLER:

One calls these "laying workers;" it is an illness in the colony.

DR. STEINER:

In practical bee-keeping it is of no great importance, but by special feeding, the colony is able to make an egg-laying bee out of an ordinary worker-bee. It is a kind of illness. The colony is a unity in itself, and the colony is then ill. If you take a goose and overfeed it till the liver is over-developed, then the whole organism is ill. If a worker-bee becomes a layer of eggs, it is an over-developed worker-bee, but the whole colony must then be regarded as ill.

Perhaps some other questions may occur to you later, we can then return to them. Meanwhile I will add a few words in reply to the question asked by Herr Dollinger.

One can clearly distinguish those insects that in the wider sense are bee-like, the bees, wasps, and ants. These small creatures are related to one another, and I have already told you the interesting story of the gall-wasps which deposit their eggs in trees and similar places. I explained further how a kind of inner preparation of honey takes place through these wasps. There are also other kinds of wasps beside these gall-wasps, which more closely resemble the bees as they make a kind of honey-comb. There is, for example, an interesting wasp which builds in the following way: when it finds a rather stiff leaf on some branch, it fetches small particles which it bites off from the bark of neighbouring trees, or some similar substance; these it permeates with its saliva, and then proceeds to build a number of small stalks which it attaches to the leaf. When it has completed these attachments the wasp goes on working, mixing these substances with saliva and building on to these stalks something very similar to the single cell of the honey-comb. On a closer inspection of this substance it is, however, seen to be different. Honey-comb, as you know, is made of wax, but when you take a piece of this wasp-comb it has a greyish colour, it is very much like what we manufacture as paper. It is actually a kind of paper-pulp. Then second, third, fourth pieces are added and hung up there.

When eggs have been deposited in these cells, they are covered over, but during the time of laying, the wasp in a most curious way, makes a kind of loop out of its paper, (Diagram 15) and then again a kind of covering with an opening at one side for a flight hole, so that the wasps can go in and out and attend to these little cells, Then more rows of cells are added, covered in, again a loop, a cover and a flight hole, and so on, till there may be quite a long cone, like a fir-cone. The wasps build themselves this cone-like structure out of paper, and in its separate parts it is similar to the brood-nest of the bees. Other wasp nests are, as you know, covered in with a kind of skin, and have many and varied forms.

Just think what is happening here. If you ask me what the bee does in order to build its waxen cells, then I must say that the bee gathers what is needed from the flowers, from flowering plants, and what is of a similar nature from trees, but not concerning itself at all with the bark, or woody substances. The bee gathers only what is of the nature of the blossom, or more rarely what is leaf-like in its nature. The only time when such higher insects as the bees go to what is not of the nature of the blossom (to woody parts and such-like they do not go) is when they go after a substance that at certain times seems to be extremely tasty to them. The bees certainly do this much less than the wasps, and most especially the ants. Though the ants and wasps make use of what is lignified for their nests, they greatly relish the juices that are exuded primarily by the aphidæ. This is really most interesting. The harder the substances used by these creatures for their structures, the more do they relish not only the nectar that is within the blossom, but something that is upon the blossom or leaf, namely, the aphis. These are really noble creatures, (forgive me if I now use the language of the ants, in human speech I could not say the same), the aphis is for the ant a noble animal. It is absolutely all blossom; it is really the finest honey in the world. The wasps also have a discriminating taste for the aphis. But when we come to the ants, which are not able to build the same kind of nest as the wasps, they must set to work quite differently. The ant makes heaps of earth, and these heaps have many passages within them, a whole labyrinth of passages along which the ants then carry all they need in the way of harder substances from the bark or rind of trees. Above all, the ants like the dead parts of wood, and these materials they use to continue their building, piling it up with particles of soil. They chiefly visit the stumps of trees that have been cut down, selecting what they need from the hardened core and carrying it away for their nests.

Thus the ants use the very hardest substances, and cannot elaborate their building as far as a cellular structure. You see, the bees make use of the substances that are within the plants; with these they build their waxen cells, and are thus still dependent on the juices of the blossom for their food, on pollen for instance, and the juice-like substances in the blossom. In the case of the wasps, it is already a harder material that they need for building their cells, but it is at the same time, thinner and more brittle than honey-comb, though as a substance it is harder.

A wasp may have a fine taste for aphis, but it nevertheless feeds also, in bee-fashion, on what is contained in the plants. The ants mostly make use of such hard material that they can only make tunnels into the earth, constructing little caves without any combs or cells. They are most especially fond of the aphis; they even capture them and carry them away to their dwellings; one can find them there in the ant heaps. It is really most interesting. When you go into a village you see a row of houses, and behind them the cow-sheds where the milking cows are; the ants have just the same plan. Throughout the ant heap you will find little dwellings where the aphis are placed, for they are the milch-cows of the ants. It is only all on a minute scale, for there you will find little stalls, and the aphis are the cows. The ants go to them and stroke them with their antennæ; this is extremely pleasant to the aphis, and they exude their juice which the ants now absorb. In this juice of the aphis the ant receives the most vital element of its food, for the aphis gives up this juice when it is milked by the ant. It is really just like a cow, only the cow must be stroked much harder. The aphis are picked off the plants by the ants, and are well cared for, so that we really must say it is quite splendid for these little creatures that there should be an ant hill in the neighbourhood, and that they should be carried off by the ants and made use of in their little cow-stalls. In the wise arrangements of Nature quite a little cow market in aphis is carried on by the ants.

Thus you see, gentlemen, that the ants which make use of hard substances only for their dwellings, are no longer able to be satisfied with the pure saps of the plants for their food; they must take as food what the sap of the plant has already given to the animal. So one must say; with the bees the pure juices of the flowers suffice for food; the wasps need both the flower saps and the animal saps, hence their harder shell structure. In the case of the ants their actual food is animal sap only; hence there is no construction of cells at all. The ant has no longer the power to build cells. Even when it takes something from the flowers it still needs this substance from the little cow-stalls, otherwise it cannot live.

You see how interesting are the relationships that exist between the flowers and these creatures. The bees must use the pure saps of the flowers; the wasps, and more especially the ants, must first allow these flower juices to pass through the animal before it can serve them as nourishment. As a result of this, they are able in the building of their house, to use what is no longer the sap of the plant. There is really a very great difference between the waxen honey-comb of the bee, the paper nest of the wasp, and the structure made by the ants which can only be made from outside material, and cannot be carried to the stage of the cell. For this reason their food must be so entirely different.

On Saturday I must go to Schaffhausen, and there will be no lecture; I will let you know when the next one will take place.

LECTURE VIII.

Dornach, December 15, 1923.

GOOD morning, Gentlemen!
Today I shall continue the subject dealt with last time in answer to Herr Dollinger's question. Should anything else arise, we can consider this also.

In my answer to this question of Herr Dollinger, I spoke of the ants, and how these creatures, bees, wasps and ants are related to one another, though their modes of life are totally different. Taking our starting point from this fact, we can really learn a very great deal about the whole household of Nature, for the more one learns to understand these small creatures and their ways, the more one realises how wisely regulated their work is, and all they are able to accomplish in the realm of Nature.

Last time, I told you how the ants make their nests, how they either build up mounds of the soil itself, or gather together minute particles of decaying wood, or of wood which has become quite hard, and is no longer living; also from various other substances which they mix together. Within these ant-hills are innumerable passages, along which the ants move in procession, whole hosts of them. One sees them coming out at the entrances, searching their surroundings, and collecting what they need. Sometimes however, it happens that these creatures do not first build up a mound, but make use of something suitable they find there already. Perhaps, for instance, a tree has been cut down and the stump has been left standing; an ant colony comes along and makes a little chamber inside it, hollows it out, and makes all kind of passages with their exits. Then perhaps, they heap up a little earth, make one passage, then another, then a third and so on, and within these passages are all inter-connected.

You see, to say of all this that it is due to the instinct of the creatures may be all very well, but nothing very much has then been said, for when the creature cannot make use of a tree stump, it builds up a sand heap; when it finds a suitable tree stump, then it so arranges the matter that it saves the labour that would be needed to heap up a hillock. The small creature adjusts itself to the individual situation, and it becomes very difficult to state that this is due to instinct. This would only enable the creature to do everything in accordance with instinct; but it actually adjusts itself to the external circumstances. That is the important point.

Here, in our country, it does not frequently happen, but the further one goes south the greater nuisance do the ants become. Imagine a house, and in one corner of it, without the owner having noticed anything, the ants have gathered; they have carried in all sorts of things, particles of earth, minute fragments of wood, and in some corner that has been overlooked in cleaning, have made a small dwelling place which no one notices. From here they make passages into the kitchen, into the pantry, following the most complicated ways, and bring back all they require for food or other purposes, from the kitchen or pantry. This can happen in southern countries, and the house may be quite pervaded by a colony of ants without anyone living there knowing they are mere fellow inhabitants of the ants, until they discover by chance, or by sight, that something in the store cupboard has been nibbled, and the real source only comes to light when the passages are traced. Here again, one cannot get very far by speaking of mere instinct, for you would then have to say that Nature has given these creatures an instinct to take up their abode precisely in this very house; what they build there must be so constructed that it is adapted to this particular house.

But you see, these creatures do not work out of mere instinct; there is wisdom in what they do. If you test some individual ant, you would certainly not arrive at the conclusion that it was especially wise, for what it does when separated from the colony, or what it may be forced to do, does not reveal any special wisdom. One then begins to realise that it is not the individual ant that can reason, but the entire colony of ants as a unity; the colony of bees, for example, is wise in this sense. The separate ants of the colony have no individual intelligence, and for this reason the work is carried on by the whole colony in an extremely interesting way. There are, moreover, many other more interesting happenings within these ant-hills. There is, for instance, a kind of ant which does as follows: somewhere or other it builds on the ground a kind of wall (drawing on the board); here it is raised; here, it forms a circle on the surrounding earth, there, digs a hole. Within are the ants. Sometimes the hole is at the top, like the crater of a volcano; within are the many passages with their outlets.

Now these ants do something very peculiar. They destroy all the grasses and plants which grow round about, with the exception of one particular kind of grass. All other grasses are destroyed, even at times, all other plants. Thus, in the centre we have a kind of hillock, and all round it looks as though the ground had been very finely paved. Through the ants biting away everything, the soil has become very compact, and is very firm. There is the ant-hill, and all round it a smooth pavement, almost like asphalt, but rather lighter in colour.

The ants then search all round about and collect a certain kind of grass which they then begin to cultivate. As soon as the wind brings other seeds, they bite off the new plants the moment they begin to grow; they will not have them in the place they have made so smooth, and in all the surrounding area nothing else is permitted to grow but just this one special kind of grass. The ants have established a little property of their own, as it were, and regularly cultivate the kind of grass that best suits them; nothing else is allowed to grow there; all other plants are bitten away. The grass which is allowed to grow becomes quite different in character from the same grass where it grows further away, where, for instance, it is growing in loose soil. In the hardened soil made by the ants, the cultivated grass has quite hard seeds, as hard as stone. One can find these ant-hills. Round about them there is a regular little farm, and the ants are engaged in agriculture. Darwin, who especially observed these things, calls it so. One finds in the soil very hard seeds somewhat like small grains of maize, and when all is ready, the ants come out, bite off the tops, and carry them into their dwelling. For a while they stay inside; one does not see them, but they are very busy inside there. Whatever they have no use for, like the little stalks that were still attached to the hard seeds, they bite off, and after a time they come out again and run all about, and throw away all they do not want, keeping in their ant-hill only the hard silica-like seeds. These they partly use as food, biting them with their very hard teeth, or they use them for their building. Everything they cannot make use of they throw out. After all, we men do very much the same. These farming ants manage to provide themselves with all they need in a very fine way!

One has really to ask oneself: what is actually happening here? Actually, an entirely new kind of grass is brought into existence. These silica-hard seeds cannot be found anywhere else. They are only produced by the ants, and the ants work further upon them. What then is really happening here?

Before considering this, we will approach the question from another side. Let us go back to the wasps, among which I told you, we find creatures that deposit their eggs on the leaves, and in the bark of trees; gall-nuts are then formed out of which the young wasps emerge. But quite other things can also happen. There are certain caterpillars which look like this (drawing on the blackboard). You all know them; these caterpillars are covered with woolly hairs, with quite prickly-woolly hairs. The following can happen to these caterpillars. One or more wasps of a special kind simply insert their eggs into the caterpillar, and when the eggs mature the grubs creep out of them. Bees, and other insects of this kind, all make their first appearance as grubs, also the ants. You know how, when one clears away an ant-heap, one finds the white, so-called ants' eggs, which are given to caged birds. They are however, not eggs, but the larvæ that have crept out of the eggs. It is not correct to call them eggs.

Now when the wasp lays its eggs into the caterpillar, it is really very remarkable. As I have already told you, these grubs when they first emerge are very hungry, and there are a great number of them in the caterpillar. It is really remarkable, for if one of these grubs were to begin to eat the caterpillar's stomach, the whole affair of the wasp's development would come to an end, for the caterpillar could not live if any organ, an eye, or to do with the heart or with the digestion, were eaten into. The thing would then come to an end. But these minute wasp grubs show their intelligence by not biting into, or feeding upon any vital organ, but by eating only those organs which can be injured for quite a long time. The caterpillar does not die, it is ill; but the wasp grubs can still go on devouring it. It is most wisely arranged that the wasp grubs do not bite into anything that would fatally injure the caterpillar. Possibly, you may have seen how these larvæ emerge from inside the caterpillar when they are mature? The caterpillar has been their foster-mother, nourishing the whole brood with her own body. Now they creep out, develop further, and seek their food from the plants. When they are fully developed, the eggs are once more deposited in a similar caterpillar.

You might well say that there is something extremely clever in all this, and indeed, as I have already said, the more one observes such things, the more do they arouse one's deepest admiration. It cannot be otherwise; wonder is kindled, and one asks oneself the meaning of such things.

If one would discover their meaning, one must first say; we have the plants growing out of the earth; we have the caterpillars. Then these insects appear, and eat their fill from the flowers, and caterpillars, and then reproduce themselves. So it goes on, over and over again. To us men it seems as though the whole insect world might just as well not exist at all. Naturally, as human beings, when we see the bee, we say; the bees give us honey, therefore bee-keeping is of use to us. Very good; but this is from the point of view of man. If the bees are robbers, and merely take away the nectar from the flowers, and we men then use the honey for our food, or as a remedy, then this is all to our advantage. But from the point of view of the flowers, it looks like a mere robbery in which we, as men, take part. The question therefore, is whether from the point of view of the flowers they would say, as it were; out there are those robbers, the bees, wasps and ants who rob us of our saps; we should thrive much better if they did not take away our saps.

You see, gentlemen, this is a point of view that a man usually takes as regards the flowers. But it is not so; it is absolutely not so. The matter is entirely different. When one is looking at some flower, and an insect, let us say a bee, is sucking the juices of the flower, or from the willow blossom, one must say to oneself: how would it be for the plant if the bee, or the wasp or some other insect, did not come to suck out this nectar? How would it be then?

This is naturally a question far more difficult to answer than that of a mere robbery, for one must look deeply into the whole household of Nature. It is not possible to reach the right conclusion unless one is able to look back into the earlier stages of the earth's evolution. You see, the earth was not always the same as it is today. If the earth had always been as it is today, when we find the dead lime-stone, the dead quartz or gneiss, or mica-schist, and so on; when we find growing out of the present-day seeds, the plants, when we find the animals. If the earth had always been like this, the whole of what we see today could not exist, could not be there at all! Those who begin their science only at the point of what exists today, give themselves up to complete illusion.

He who would seek all the mysteries, all the laws of the earth in that alone wherein modern science seeks them, is as if a dweller in Mars should come down to the earth, who had no idea of living men, who only went to a mortuary and saw there the dead men. The dead could not be there at all if they had not first been living men. The inhabitant of Mars who had never seen living men, and saw only the dead, would first have to be guided to living men; then he would be able to say—" Yes, now I understand why the dead have these forms; before I did not understand this, because I did not know the living form that preceded the dead one." Thus, one must go back to earlier conditions if one would know the laws of the earth evolution. The earth had long ago a very different form; I have spoken of it as the Moon-condition, and in my book, " An Outline of Occult Science," it is also called the Moon-condition, because the present Moon is a remnant of this ancient earth. Other stages of evolution in their turn preceded this one of the Moon. The earth has transformed itself; it was originally altogether different.

Now the earth was once at such a stage that plants and insects such as we have today, did not exist at all. The matter, gentlemen, was thus; there was, let us say, something that can be compared with the earth of today. Out of this grew plant-like forms, but plant-like forms that were continually changing, that continually assumed different forms, as the clouds do, for instance. There were then such clouds in the environment of the earth, but they were not clouds like the clouds we see today, which are dead, or at least seem to be dead; they were living clouds, as living as the flowers of today. If you can imagine to yourselves that our clouds could become alive and turn a greenish colour, then you would have a picture of the plant kingdom of that time.

The scientific gentlemen of today have very strange ideas on such matters. There was recently a most ludicrous article in the newspaper. Once more a new scientific discovery had been made, quite in the modern way. It was really absurd! It was stated that if prepared in a certain way, milk was a good remedy for scurvy, a very ugly disease. Well, gentlemen, what does the scientist of today do? I have already referred to this. He analyses the milk. Then he finds that milk contains such and such chemical components. But I have also told you that one can feed mice with the chemical substances in the milk, but if one gives them these only, the mice die within a few days. Bunge's pupils confirmed this, (see previously mentioned article in the " *Schweizerische Bienen Zeitung* ") and merely said; " Well, yes, there is a life-substance in the milk, as also in honey, Vitamin." You remember, as I said before, one might just as well say " poverty comes from being poor," as say what is said here, " there is Vitamin in it."

Well gentlemen, an important discovery has been made; there are various substances in milk, that have very complicated names and milk when prepared in a special way, is a remedy for scurvy. Then in a truly learned way investigations were made to see whether the scurvy could be cured if one gave the scurvy patients only all the things with the learned names that were contained in the milk. They were not in the least cured by any of the component substances. But when all of these were present (in the specially prepared milk) then the scurvy was cured. No single component by itself cured, only the whole together. Well says the scientist to himself; what remains over when one subtracts all the components? What then remains over? For now he eliminates them all. He does not admit that these components have an etheric body, he reckons them all out, and what remains?

The "*Vitamin!*" The vitamin which must be what cures the scurvy is not to be found among the component parts. Where then is it? So now they make this fine tale—it must be in the water of the milk! Therefore, the remedy for scurvy is the water! This is really absurd, but it is a learned affair today. For if water is to contain vitamin, then with our learning we should arrive up there in the clouds. We should have to look around us and say: "Water is everywhere and vitamin is in the water." But then we would be at the stage at which the earth once was. Only today, it is no longer so. Plant-life was there, a living plant covering, and this living covering of plants was fertilised from all directions from the environment. There were then no separate animals, no wasps for instance, but from the surrounding regions there came a substance which had an animal-like nature. Our earth was once in a condition of which one could say that it was surrounded by clouds that had plant-life within them; from the periphery, other clouds approached and fertilised them; these clouds had an animal nature. From cosmic spaces came the animal nature; from the earth the essence of plant-being rose upwards.

All this has changed. The plants have become our clearly outlined flowers which grow out of the earth, no longer forming great clouds. But within the plants there remains a longing to receive an influence from without. Here we have a rose growing out of the earth; here a rose petal, here another, then a third and so on. Now comes a wasp. This wasp immediately bites a piece out of the rose petal, carries it off to its nest, and uses it for building, or gives it as food to its young. A piece of the rose petal is simply bitten out by the wasp, and carried there, Well, as I said before, our rose bushes are no longer clouds: they have become sharply defined things. But what once lived within them, what was once united with all that entered in as the essence of animal life, this has remained behind within the rose leaves and blossoms. It is there within them. In every rose leaf is something which must of necessity be in some way fertilised from without, from the whole environment.

You see, gentlemen, what the flowers need, what they actually need, is a substance that also plays an important part in the human body. When you study the human body the most diverse substances are found in it. But everywhere within the human body these substances are transformed into something which, in certain quantities, is always present within the human body which has need of it. This substance is formic acid.

If you go to an ant-hillock, and collect some ants and squeeze them, you get a juice. This juice contains formic acid and a little alcohol. It is inside the ants. But this juice is also very finely distributed over your body. Whatever you eat during your life time is always transformed into formic acid, not of course, exclusively, for there are other substances also, but in small quantities. This formic acid permeates your whole body. When you are ill, and have not sufficient formic acid within you, it is a serious matter for your body, for it then has a tendency, just because you have not enough formic acid within you, (and here I come once more to Herr Müller's question, in answer to it) your body has a tendency to become gouty, or rheumatic. It develops too much uric acid, and too little formic acid. The ants also have in their bodies this substance that the human body needs. This formic acid, gentlemen, is indeed something that is made use of throughout nature. You actually cannot find any bark of any tree that does not contain some formic acid. Formic acid is everywhere in the tree, just as it is in the human body. In every leaf, everywhere there must be formic acid.

But not only formic acid must be there, but also what is closely akin to it, and later becomes the bee poison. All these insects contain a certain substance within them which is poisonous. If one is stung by a bee, one gets inflammation; if one is stung by a wasp, it is sometimes even worse. This business of wasp stings can be pretty bad. Brehm describes how these insects can play bad tricks on men and animals.

It happened that a young cow-herd had taken a large number of cows out to graze, and the pasture was full of wasp nests. The cow-herd's dog ran about; suddenly the cow-herd's dog goes mad, rushes round like a mad dog, and no one knows what has happened. As fast as it can the dog rushes to a neighbouring stream, flings itself into the water, and shakes and shakes itself. The lad was much disturbed by this, and goes to the rescue of the dog. He does not jump into the water, but tries to help it from the bank. Most unluckily he steps on a nest, as the dog had probably done before, and the wasps sting him too, and he begins to rush about like a madman, and finally jumps into the water. And now, because the dog has vanished, and the cow-herd has vanished, confusion arises in the herd of cows. The cows which tread on nests also get stung, and behave as though mad. Finally, most of the herd are in the stream also—as if they were all mad.

You see, insect stings can do one a very bad turn. All these creatures have poisons in them; even an ant stings one, and causes a little inflammation because it injects some formic acid into the wound. This formic acid, moreover, is present in all living things in a right dilution. If there were no ants, bees and wasps, which are the preparers of these poisons, what would happen?

Truly, gentleman, the same thing would happen that would also come to pass in the propagation of the human race if all the men were beheaded, and only women were left on the earth. Humanity could not then continue to exist, for the male semen would no longer be there. Well, these creatures all have the semen in addition, but they none-the-less need what comes from these poisons for their existence, for these poisons have remained over from what was once in the whole environment. In the finest state of dilution, bee poison, wasp poison, ant poison, once descended upon the plants from cosmic spaces, and the remnants are still present today. So when you see a bee sitting on some willow-tree or on some flower, you must not say: the insect only wants to rob the flower of something; rather must you say: when the little bee sits there and sucks, the flower is so content that it lets its sap flow to the spot where the bee sucks. While the bee is taking something from the flower, bee or wasp poison flows from the bee to the flower. From the wasp, the wasp poison flows, and more especially when the ant attacks the tree stump which no longer has life, formic acid flows in. If the ant visits a flower, then the sap of the flower unites with the formic acid. This is necessary.

If these things did not happen, if bees, wasps and ants did not exist and continually attack the plants and bite into them, then the necessary formic acid, the necessary poisons, would not flow into the flowers, and the plants would in time die out.

You see, substances such as are usually called life-substances, are highly valued by man; yet it is precisely only these substances that are truly life-substances. If one has deadly nightshade, within it is a poison, a very powerful one. But what is the deadly nightshade? It collects spirituality from the world's environment. Poisons are gatherers of what is spiritual; for this reason they are healing remedies. Fundamentally speaking, the flowers sicken through the life-substances, and the little bees, and wasps and ants, work continually as small physicians bringing to the flowers the formic acid they need, and at the same moment, healing their sickness. Thus all is once more healed.

The bees, wasps and ants are not mere robbers, for in the same moment they bring life to the plants.

It is even the same with the caterpillars which would also die out, and none would remain after a time. You will probably say no great harm would be done if all the caterpillars were to disappear; but in their turn the birds feed on them. Throughout the whole of Nature there are these inner relationships. When we see, for example, how the ants permeate everything with their formic acid, we look into the whole household of Nature and its splendour. Everywhere things happen that are essential for the maintenance of life, and of the world.

You see, here is a tree, and the tree has bark. The bark decays when I cut down the tree; then it moulders. People say: "Well, let it rot away." Just try to imagine all that moulders away in the forests, fallen leaves and so on, within the course of the year! Men are willing to let it all rot away, but Nature orders it otherwise. Everywhere there are ant-heaps, and from these ant-heaps formic acid enters into the soil of the forest. When you have both forest soil and an ant-heap, it is the same as if you take a glass of water and add a drop of something else to it; the whole contents are at once affected. If you put in salt, all the water is at once made salty. If you have an ant-heap then the formic acid goes in the same moment into the forest soil, and all the soil which is already decaying is saturated with this formic acid.

It is not only into the inner parts of the living plants, and into the still living caterpillars that formic acid penetrates when the bee sits on the flower, and the flower absorbs what it receives from the bee. All these things can only be learned by means of spiritual science; the other kind of science is only concerned with what the bee takes away from the flowers. But the bees would never have been able to sit for thousands of years on the flowers had they not fostered them in the act of biting into them.

So it is also with the lifeless substances of the woods. Even physical science as it is today, concludes that the earth will one day be quite dead. It would indeed be so, for a state of things would eventually come about when decay would prevail, when the earth would be dead. That this will not be so, is because wherever the earth decays it is in the same moment penetrated by all that is yielded up by the bees, wasps and ants. The bees, it is true, give it only to the living flowers, the wasps for the most part also to the living plants. But the ants give what they hand over in the formic acid directly to what is mouldering and dead; in a certain degree they rouse it to life, in this way doing their part that the earth in its decaying substances shall still retain life. Well may one say that wonder is awakened at the activity of the spirit in all things, but when one can approach it more nearly, then one realises it has immense significance.

Let us look once more at those farming ants which cultivate their little field, and change the character of the plants they grow there. Truly, gentlemen, a man could not nourish himself with what grows there, for if a man were to eat those little rice grains that are as hard as silica, he would first get strange illnesses because he would have too much formic acid inside him, and in addition to this, so injure his teeth that for a time the dentists would be kept busy. At last, he would die wretchedly, because of these silica-hard rice-grains which had been thus developed.

But the ant-heap would say: when we ants go out into nature and suck that out of the plants which is everywhere there, then we get far too little formic acid, and can give far too little formic acid to the earth. Let us therefore, select the plants which we can cultivate so that they get quite hard, stony hard, and then we can get plenty of formic acid from this hardness. So these farming ants do this that they may get the greatest possible amount of formic acid. It is these ants again that give back so much formic acid to the earth. That is the connection. From this you can see that poisons when they cause inflammation, or the like, are also perpetual remedies for the holding back of the processes of death. One can say, it is precisely the bee that is of great importance in this regard, that all may be preserved within the flowers; there is a great affinity between the bees and the flowers.

This preservation actually shows that every time the insects are developing their activities on the earth, the earth is, as it were, quickened by their poison. This is the spiritual relationship. If anyone asks what are the spiritual relationships, I never like merely to say they are so and so; I give the facts, and from the facts you can judge for yourselves whether they have significance or no. The facts are such that one sees significance everywhere. But the people who call themselves scientists today, do not tell one so. In life this has certain effects. In our country this is perhaps less taken into account, but when you go further south, the simple folk, the peasants, will often say out of a kind of instinctive knowledge; one must not destroy these ant-heaps, for they prevent the mould from becoming harmful. Those who are still wiser, will say something quite different if you walk with them through the forest, and especially where trees have been cut down and young trees are growing up. Then these people who are wise in their noses, not in their top-story (one can be wise also in one's nose) when these people go where the trees have been felled and young trees are being cared for, they will say: " Here, it will all go well; it does not smell so mouldy as it often does; there must be an ant-heap near, and it is proving its usefulness." These people smell this; they are clever with their noses. Much homely and useful knowledge is derived from a clever nose! Unfortunately, modern civilisation only regards the cultivation of the brain, and rejects all that is instinctive; instinct has become merely a word.

Creatures like the bees know all this collectively, as a colony, as an ant-heap; it comes about by a kind of sense of smell. As I said before, much that is instinctive knowledge may come from a cleverness of the nose.

Well, gentlemen, we shall continue the subject next week Today, I wished to say that the bees, wasps and ants do not only rob Nature, but help to make it possible for Nature to live and thrive.

LECTURE IX.

Dornach, December 22, 1923.

GOOD morning, Gentlemen!
We should perhaps say something further on the subject of Herr Dollinger's question. He asked, on your behalf, for it is probably of interest to you all, what the spiritual relationship is between the hosts of insects which, fluttering about, approaches the plants and what is to be found in the plants. I told you yesterday, for we began to answer this question last time, that all around us there is not only oxygen and nitrogen, but that throughout Nature there is intelligence, truly intelligence. No one is surprised if one says that we breathe in the air, for air is everywhere, and science today is so widely included in all the school books that everyone knows that air is everywhere, and that we breathe it in. All the same I have known country people who thought this a fantastic idea, because they did not know the air is everywhere; in the same way there are people today who do not know that intelligence is everywhere. They consider it fantastic if one says that just as we breathe in the air with our lungs, so do we breathe in intelligence, for example, through our nose, or through our ear. I have already given instances in which you could see that there is intelligence everywhere.

We have been speaking of an especially interesting chapter of natural science, of the bees, wasps and ants. There is, may be, little in Nature which permits us to look so deeply into Nature herself, as the activities of the insects; the insects are strange creatures, and they have still many a secret to disclose.

It is interesting that we should be discussing the insects just at the time of the centenary of the famous observer of insects, Jean Henri Fabre, who was born on December 23, one hundred years ago, and whose life time coincides with the age of materialism. Fabre therefore interpreted everything materialistically, but he also brought to light an enormous number of facts. It is therefore quite natural that we should remember him today when we speak of the insects.

I should like to begin with, to give you an example of a species of insect which will interest you in connection with the bees. The work of the bees is perfected to a very high degree, but the most remarkable thing about the bee is really not that it produces honey but, that it produces the marvellous structure of the honey-comb entirely out of its own being. The material it makes use of, it must itself bring into the hive, but the bee actually works in such a way that it does not use this material directly, but completely transforms it, completely transforms what it brings into the hive. The bee works from out of its own being.

Now there is a kind of bee which does not work in this way, but shows, precisely in its work, what immense intelligence there is in the whole of Nature. Let us consider this bee; it is commonly called the wood-bee, and is not so valued as the domestic bee, because it is mostly rather a nuisance. We will consider this wood-bee at its work.

It is a tremendously industrious little creature, a creature which in order to live—not the individual bee, but the whole species —must do a terrific amount of work. This bee searches out such wood as is no longer on a living tree, but has been made into something. One finds the wood-bee which I shall presently describe, with its nest in a place where wooden rails, or posts have been driven in and the wood is therefore apparently dead. The nests can usually be found in wooden rails or posts, in garden benches, or garden doors, in fact wherever one has made use of wood. Here the wood-bee makes its nest, but it does so in a very singular way.

Imagine to yourselves a post (Diagram 16.) The wood is no longer part of a tree. The wood-bee comes along and first of all bores a sloping passage from outside. When it has got inside, when it has bored out a kind of passage, it starts boring in quite a new direction. It makes a little ring-like hollow, then flies off and collects all manner of things from round about, and lines out the hollow with these. Having finished the lining, it deposits an egg which will develop into a larva. This is now inside the hollow. When the egg has been placed there, the little bee makes a covering over it, in the centre of which there is a hole. Now it begins to bore again above the cover, and makes a second little hollow for the second bee that is to creep out, and having lined it and left a hole it lays another egg. The wood-bee continues in this way till it has constructed ten or twelve of these superimposed dwellings; in each one there is an egg.

You see, gentlemen, the larva can now mature in this piece of wood. The bee puts some food next to the larva which first eats what has been prepared for it, and grows till it is ready to creep out. First we have the time when the grub becomes a cocoon, then it is transformed into a winged bee which is to fly out. Inside there it is so arranged (see Diagram 16), that the larva now developed can fly out at the right moment. When the time comes that the larva has developed, has turned into a cocoon, and then into a complete insect, then it is so arranged that it is able to fly out through the passage. The skill employed has enabled the fully formed insect to fly out through the passage that was first bored.

Well and good, but the second insect that is a little younger, now emerges, and the third that is still younger; because the mother insect had first to make these dwelling-places, the creatures would not find any outlet, the situation would be fatal to the larvæ in the upper chambers, they would slowly die. But the mother insect prevents this by laying the eggs so that when the young larva creeps out, it finds this other hole which I described, and lets itself down there, and flies out. The third creature comes down through the two holes and so on. Because each insect that comes out *later* is matured later, it does not hinder the one below it which had emerged earlier. The times are never the same, for the earlier has always already flown out.

You see, gentlemen, the whole nest is so wisely planned that one can only wonder at it.

Today when men imitate mechanically, the things they copy are often of this kind, but as a rule they are far less cleverly constructed. Things that exist in Nature are extremely wisely made, and one must really say that there is intelligence in them, real intelligence. One could give hundreds and thousands of examples of the way the insects build, of the way they set about their tasks, and how intelligence lives within these things. Think how much intelligence there is in all I have already told you about the farming ants which establish their own farm, and plan everything with wonderful intelligence.

But in considering these insects, the bees, wasps and ants, we were at the same time dealing with another matter. I told you that these creatures all have a poisonous substance within them, and that this poisonous substance is also, if given in the right dose, an excellent remedy. Bee-poison is an excellent remedy; wasp-poison is the same, and the formic acid secreted by the ants is a most especially good remedy. But as I have already pointed out, this formic acid which we find when we go to an ant-heap and take out a few ants and crush them, these ants have the formic acid inside them; by crushing them we get the formic acid. It is found more especially in the ants.

But gentlemen, if you knew how much, (of course, comparatively speaking,) how much formic acid there is in this hall, you would be greatly astonished. You might say, surely we are not to look for an ant-heap in some corner! But all of you, as many as are sitting here, are really yourselves a kind of ant-heap, for everywhere in your limbs, muscles and other tissues, in the heart and lung and liver tissues, above all in the tissues of the spleen, everywhere there is formic acid; certainly, it is not so concentrated as in the ant-heap, nevertheless, you are quite filled with formic acid. It is a highly remarkable fact.

Why do we have formic acid in our bodies? One must be able to recognise when a man has too little of it. If someone seems ill, and people are mostly a little ill, he might have one or another of a hundred different illnesses which externally, would seem similar. One must know what is really the matter with him; if he is pale or has no appetite, these are only external symptoms. One must find out what exactly is wrong with him. In many cases, the trouble might well be that he is not enough of an ant-heap in himself, that he is producing too little formic acid. Just as formic acid is produced in the ant-heap, so in the human body, in all its organs, especially in the spleen, formic acid must be vigourously produced. When a man produces too little formic acid, one must give him a preparation, a remedy with which one can help him to produce sufficient formic acid. One must learn to observe what happens to a man who has too little formic acid in him. Such observations can only be made by those who have a true knowledge of human nature. One must make a picture of what is happening in the soul of a man who, to begin with, had enough formic acid, and later, has too little. It is a singular thing, but a man will tell you the correct thing about his illness, if you ask him in the right way. Suppose, for instance, you had a man who tells you: "Why, good gracious, a few months ago I had ever so many good ideas, and I could think them out well. Now I cannot do so any longer; if I want to remember anything, I cannot do so." This is often a much more important symptom than any external examination can give. What is done today is of course justifiable, one must do these things. Today one can test the urine for albumen, or sugar and so on; one gets quite interesting results. But in certain circumstances, it can be far more important when a man tells you something of the kind I have just told you. When a man tells you something of this kind, one must of course, learn other things about him also, but one can discover that the formic acid in his body has recently become insufficient.

Well, anyone who still thinks only of externals, might say: "This man has too little formic acid, I will squeeze out some formic acid, or get it in some other way, and give him the right dose." This could be done for a certain time, but the patient would come to you and say it has done him no good at all. What then is the matter? It really has not helped him at all. It was quite correct; the man had too little formic acid, and he has been given formic acid, but it did him no good. What is the reason? You see, when you examine further, you come to this point. In the one case formic acid has done no good, in another case, it has continued to do good. Well presently one learns to see the difference. Those who are helped by formic acid, will usually show mucus in the lungs. Those who got no help from it, will show mucus in the liver, kidneys, or in the spleen.

It is very interesting. It is therefore a very different matter if the lung, for example, lacks formic acid, or the liver. The difference is that the formic acid which is in the ant-heap, can immediately take effect upon the lung. The liver cannot do anything with the formic acid, it can make no use of it at all.

Something further now comes in question. When you discover that a man's liver, or more especially his intestines are not quite in good order, and if one gives him formic acid it does not help him, though he actually has not enough of it, then one must give him oxalic acid. One must take wood-sorrel, or the common-clover that grows in the fields, extract the acid, and give him this.

Thus you see, anyone with lung trouble must be given formic

acid, whereas if the trouble is in the liver, or the intestines, he must be given oxalic acid. The remarkable thing is that the man to whom one has given oxalic acid, will before long himself change the oxalic acid into formic acid. The main point therefore is, that one does not simply introduce such things into a man's body, but that one knows what the organism can bring about by means of its own resourses. When you introduce formic acid into the organism, it says;—"This is not for me; I want to be active, I cannot work with ready-made formic acid, I cannot take it up into my lungs." Naturally, the formic acid has gone into the stomach; from there it finally passes into the intestines. Then the human body wants to be active, and say, as it were: "What am I supposed to do now? I am not to make formic acid myself, for formic acid is given me; have I to send this from here up into my lungs? This I shall not do." The body wants oxalic acid, and from this it produces formic acid.

Yes, gentlemen, life consists of activity, not of substances, and it is most important to recognise that life does not merely consist of eating cabbages and turnips, but of what the human body must do when cabbages and turnips are put into it.

You can see from this what strange relationships exist in Nature. Outside there, are the plants, The clover is merely especially characteristic, for oxalic acid is to be found in all the plants; in clover it is present in greater quantities, that is why it is mentioned. But just as formic acid is everywhere in Nature and everywhere in the human body, so also is there oxalic acid everywhere in Nature and in the human body.

There is something further that is very interesting. Suppose you take a retort, such as are used in chemical laboratories. You make a flame under it, and put into the retort some oxalic acid—it is like salty, crumbly ashes. You then add the same quantity of glycerine, mix the two together, and heat it. The mixture will then distil here, (Diagram 17) and I can condense what I get here (Diagram 17). At the same time I notice air is escaping at this point. Here it escapes. When I now examine this escaping air, I find it is carbonic acid. Thus carbonic acid is escaping here, and here, where I condense (Diagram 17) I get formic acid. In here, I had oxalic acid and glycerine. The glycerine remains, the rest goes over there, the fluid formic acid dropping down and the carbonic acid giving out the air.

Well, gentlemen, when you consider this whole matter thoroughly, you will be able to say: suppose, that instead of the retort we had here the human liver or let us say some human or animal tissue, some animal abdominal organ, liver, spleen or something of this nature. By way of the stomach I introduce oxalic acid. The body already possesses something of the nature of glycerine. I have then in the intestines oxalic acid and glycerine. What happens?

Now look at the human mouth, for there the carbonic acid comes out, and downwards from the lungs formic acid everywhere drops in the human body in the direction of the organs. Thus everything I have drawn here we have also in our own bodies. Within our own bodies we unceasingly transform oxalic acid into formic acid.

And now imagine to yourself the plants spread out over the surface of the earth. Everywhere in the plants is oxalic acid. And now think of the insects; with the insects all this occurs in the strangest way. First think of the ants; they go to the plants, to all that decays in the plants, and everywhere there is oxalic acid, and these creatures make formic acid from it in the same way that a man does. Formic acid is everywhere present.

The materialist looks out into the air and says:—Yes, in the air there is nitrogen and oxygen. But gentlemen, in very, very minute quantities there is also always some formic acid present, because the insects flutter through the air. On the one hand we have man. Man is a little world; he produces formic acid in himself, and continually fills his breath with formic acid. But in the great world without, in the place of what happens in man, there is the host of insects. The great breath of air that surrounds the whole earth is always permeated with formic acid which is the transformed oxalic acid of the plants. Thus it is.

If one rightly observes and studies the lower part of the human body with its inner organs, the stomach, liver, kidneys and the spleen, and further within, the intestines, it is actually the case that oxalic acid is perpetually being changed into formic acid, this formic acid passes with the inbreathed air into all parts of the body. So it is within man.

On the earth the plants are everywhere, and everywhere the innumerable hosts of insects hover above them. Below is the oxalic acid; the insects flutter towards it, and from their biting into the plants formic acid arises and fills the air. Thus we perpetually inhale this formic acid out of the air. What the wasps have is a poison similar to formic acid, but somewhat different; what the bees have in the poison of their sting, though actually it pervades their whole body, is likewise a transformed, a sublimated formic acid.

Looking at the whole, one has this picture. One says to oneself: we look at the insects, ants, wasps and bees. Externally, they are doing something extremely clever. Why are they doing this? If the ant had no formic acid it would do quite stupidly all that I have described as so beautiful. Only because the ants are so constituted that they can produce formic acid, only because of this, does all that they accomplish appear so intelligent and wise. This also applies to the wasps and the bees.

Have we not every reason to say (for we produce this formic acid in ourselves): In Nature there is intelligence everywhere; it comes through the formic acid. In ourselves also there is intelligence everywhere because we have formic acid within us. This formic acid could not be in existence had not the oxalic acid first been there. The little creatures hovering over the plants see to it that the oxalic acid is changed into formic acid, that it is metamorphosed.

One only fully understands these things when one asks: How is it then with the oxalic acid? Oxalic acid is essential for all that has life. Wherever there is life, there is oxalic acid, an etheric body. The etheric body brings it about that the oxalic acid is renewed. But the oxalic acid never becomes a formic acid that can be used by the human or animal organism unless it is first transformed by an astral body from oxalic into formic acid. The formic acid which I here extracted from the oxalic acid, is of no use at all to the human or animal organism. It is an illusion to think it can be of use; it is dead. The oxalic acid which is produced in man, and through the insects is *living*, and arises everywhere where sensation, or something of the nature of the soul is present.

Man must produce formic acid in himself if he wishes to bring forth something of the nature of the soul out of the mere life-processes of the lower body where the oxalic acid prevails. Then, in the formic acid of the breath there lives the soul quality that rises up to, and can be active in the head. The soul needs this transformation in man of the oxalic into formic acid.

What then is actually happening when oxalic acid is changed into formic acid? You see, the first thing that I told you can show us this. The wood-bee which I described, is especially interesting for it works in wood that is no longer living. If this wood-bee could not make use of the wood in the right way, it would seek a dwelling place elsewhere. It does not make its nest in a tree, but in decaying wood, and where rails and posts begin to rot away; there it makes a nest and lays its eggs.

If you study the connection of the decaying wood and the wood-bee, wasps, etc., then you find that similar processes of decay constantly take place in the human body. If this process of decay goes too far, the body dies. Man must constantly carry on in himself what happens externally; he must build up cells, and this he can only do by transforming all that is plant-like within him and permeated with oxalic acid; he must change all this into formic acid so that all is permeated with formic acid.

You will say: What significance has all this for Nature?

Let us imagine one of these decaying posts or rails. Should one of these wood bees never discover it, a man would certainly not regret it, for these bees increase quickly, and the post they have hollowed out would fall down the following year. Men may not appreciate this, but Nature finds it good, for if there were none of these creatures all woody substances would gradually crumble into dust, and would become entirely useless. The wood in which the wood-bees have worked does not perish in dust, it is given new life. From all this decaying wood that is quickened a little by the wood-bee, or by other insects, much arises which rescues our earth from complete decay, from being scattered as dust in cosmic space; our earth can live on it because it has been quickened by the insects. As men we breathe in formic acid; in Nature the formic acid is prepared by the insects from the oxalic acid of the plants, and so works that the earth renews its life.

Consider the connection. We have man, and we have the earth. Let us take first a young child, for a young child readily transforms the oxalic acid of the lower organism into formic acid. The organs of a young child are sufficiently supplied with formic acid; the human soul develops in the child. We have the formic acid as the basis for the soul and spirit. But when a man grows old and is unable to develop sufficient formic acid, then the soul and spirit must take leave of the body. Formic acid draws the soul and spirit to the body; otherwise the soul and spirit must leave it. It is deeply interesting.

If for instance you observe a man who has developed a number of independent inner processes, you will find that it is formic acid that helps him to master these independent inner processes. The right relationship is then brought about between the astral body and the physical body which were hindered by these independent processes in the body. Formic acid is always needed as the right basis for the soul and spirit. When the body has too little it decays, and can no longer retain the soul; the body ages and the soul must leave it.

We have then, man on the one side and Nature on the other side. In Nature formic acid is continually being prepared from oxalic acid, so that the earth may always be surrounded not only by oxygen and nitrogen, but by formic acid also. It is formic acid that prevents the earth from dying every year, gives it each year renewed life. What is beneath the earth longs as seed for the formic acid above, for renewal of its life. Every winter the spirit of the earth actually strives to take leave of the earth. The spirit of the earth benumbs the earth in winter, to quicken it again in spring. This happens because what waits as seed beneath the earth draws near to the formic acid which has arisen through the whole intercourse of the insect world and the plant world throughout the preceding year. The seeds do not merely grow in oxygen, nitrogen and carbon, but in formic acid; this formic acid stimulates them in their turn to develop oxalic acid, so that once more the formic acid of the succeeding year may come into existence.

Just as in man formic acid can be the basis for his soul and spirit, so the formic acid which is spread out in the cosmos can be the basis for the soul and spirit of the earth. Thus we can say that for the earth also, formic acid is the basis for earth-soul and earth-spirit. (see Diagram 18).

You see, it is actually much more difficult to telegraph in a district where there are no ant-heaps, for the electricity and magnetism necessary for telegraphing depend on formic acid. When the telegraph wires go through towns where there are no ant-heaps, it is from the fields outside the town that power must be collected to enable the electric streams to pass through the towns. Naturally, the formic acid is present in the air of the towns also.

Thus we can say: What is within man as production of formic acid, is also outside in external Nature. Man is a little world, and between birth and death he is able to produce formic acid from oxalic acid. When he can no longer do so, his body dies. He must once more take a body which in childhood can develop formic acid from oxalic acid in the right way. In Nature the process is unbroken, winter-summer, winter-summer; ever the oxalic acid

If one watches beside a dying man one really has the feeling that in dying, he first tries whether his body is still able to develop formic acid. When he can no longer accomplish this, death takes place. Man passes into the spiritual world, for he can no longer inhabit his body. Hence, we say that a man dies at a given moment. A long time then passes, and he returns to take another is undergoing transformation into formic acid.
body; between whiles, he is in the spiritual worlds.

Well, gentlemen, as I told you, when a young Queen slips out in the hive, something disturbs the bees. Previously they had lived in their twilight world; now they see the young Queen begin to shine. What is connected with this shining? It is connected with the fact that the young Queen robs the old Queen of the power of the bee poison. The whole departing swarm feels this fear, this fear that they will no longer possess a sufficiency of poison, will no longer be able to protect, or save themselves. They go away just as the human soul goes away at death when it can no longer find the formic acid it needs: so too, the older bees go away when there is not sufficient formic acid, bee poison, in the hive.

So now, if one watches the swarm, still indeed visible to us, yet it is like the human soul when it must desert the body. It is a majestic picture, this departing swarm. Just as the human soul takes leave of the body, so when the young Queen is there, the old Queen with her company leaves the hive; one can truly see in the flying swarm an image of the departing human soul.

How truly magnificent all this is! But the human soul has not carried the process so far as to develop its forces into actual small creatures; the tendency to do this is nevertheless there. We have something within us that we wish to transform into tiny creatures, into bacilli and bacteria—into minute bees. But we suppress this tendency that we may be wholly men. The swarm of bees is not a whole man. The bees cannot find their way into a spiritual world, it is we who must bring them into a new incarnation as a new colony.

This is, gentlemen, directly an image of re-incarnating man. Anyone who is able to observe this, has an immense respect for these swarming bees with their Queen, for this swarm which behaves as it does because it desires to go into the spiritual world; but for this it has become too physical. Therefore these bees gather themselves together, and become like one body; they wish to be together, they wish to leave the world. Whereas they otherwise fly about, now they settle on some branch or bush, clustering together quietly as though they wish to vanish away, to go into the spiritual world.

If we now bring them back, if we help them by placing them in a new hive, then they can once more become a complete colony.

We must say that the insects teach us the very highest things of Nature. This is why in bygone times men were always enlightened when they looked at the plants; they possessed an instinctive knowledge of these things of which I have been speaking to you, a knowledge completely lost to modern science. These men observed the plants in their own way. When people today bring into their houses a branch of a fir-tree for a Christmas tree, they remind themselves that all that is outside in Nature can also work in our human and social life. This fir branch from which the Christmas tree is made should become for us a symbol of love. It is commonly thought that the Christmas tree is a very old custom, but the fir-tree has only been so used for 150 to 200 years. In earlier times this custom did not exist, but another plant was made use of at Christmas time. When the Christmas plays, for example, were performed in the villages, even in the 15th and 16th Centuries, there was always a man who went round to announce them who carried a kind of Christmas tree in his hand. This was a branch of the juniper that has such wonderful berries; the juniper was the Christmas tree. This was because these juniper berries, so greatly loved by the birds, contain something of that poison which must pervade all that is earthly, so that this earthly may rise again in the spirit. Just as the ants give to the wood, or the wood-bee to the decaying posts, so when the birds eat the juniper berries every morning, a certain acid, though a weaker one, is developed. People in olden days knew this instinctively, and said to themselves: " In winter when the birds come to eat the juniper berries the earth is quickened through the juniper tree." It was for them a symbol of the quickening of the earth through Christ.

Thus we can say: When we observe things in the right way, we see how the processes of Nature are actually images and symbols of what happens in human life. These men of olden times watched the birds on the juniper trees with the same love with which we look at the little cakes and gifts on the Christmas tree. To them the juniper tree was a kind of Christmas tree which they carried into their houses; the juniper became a kind of Christmas tree.

As you are now all of you especially hard at work, we must close. I did not want today's lecture to end without touching on a subject of real importance. I have therefore spoken of the juniper tree which can truly be regarded as a kind of Christmas tree, and which is the same for the birds as the blossoms for the bees, the wood for the ants, and for the wood-bees and insects in general.

In conclusion, I should like to wish you a happy, cheerful Christmas Festival, and one which may uplift your hearts.

APPENDIX.

Extract from a Lecture given by Dr. Steiner at Dornach, November 10, 1923.

.... THERE is something that exists in Nature which is like a head without a bony skull; something in which the same forces work from outside that work within the head.

Now a bee-hive is similar to a head which is open on all sides. What the bees do is really the same, only in the outer world, as the head carries out in man's inner organisation, only in the hive it is not cut off and separated, but operates, and is brought about from without. Thus we have in the bee-hive under external spiritual influences, the same that in the head is under inner spiritual influences.

In the hive we have also honey, and when as grown-up human beings we take it and eat it, the honey supplies us with what we need in the way of formative forces, from outside. It is the same force which milk supplies for the head during babyhood. So long as we are little children we strengthen these formative forces in the head when we take milk. At a later age we also need formative forces, and we must therefore eat honey. We do not need to take a large quantity, it is merely a question of absorbing the forces within the honey.

Extract from a Lecture given at Dornach, December 30, 1923.

WE can actually find certain places in Nature where the physical forces of the earth enter into the midst of the etheric forces that stream in from all sides. You may imagine albumen, for instance, as a substance present in the physical earth. So long as sulphur, carbon, oxygen, nitrogen and hydrogen are in any way chemically recognisable in it, the albumen is in fact subject to the earthly forces. But the moment it enters the sphere of the reproductive process, it is lifted out of the physical forces. The forces of the circumference of the universe begin to work upon it in its disorganised condition. A new albumen comes into being as an image of the whole universe.

But you see, sometimes the following situation arises. The dis-organisation, the breaking down of the albumen cannot go far enough. You may have albuminous substance of this kind in connection with some animal, for example. For reproduction to take place, it must be possible for it to be broken down completely, so that it may submit itself to the forces of the whole Cosmos. But the animal is somehow prevented from delivering over, for purposes of reproduction, such albuminous substance as would be able straightforwardly to submit itself to the whole macrocosm. To be capable of reproduction, albuminous substance must in fact, submit itself to the whole macrocosm. But the animal is in this case, somehow unable to form albuminous substance capable of reproduction without further assistance. This is the case with the gall-wasp. What then does the gall-wasp do? It lays its egg in some part of a plant. Again and again you may find these galls, in oaks, or in other trees where the gall-wasp or fly lays her eggs. In a leaf, for example, you see these remarkable formations. Within each one is the egg of a gall-wasp. Why is the egg of the gall-fly laid in an oak-leaf so that the oak-apple arises in which the egg is enclosed, and now capable of development? Could it not have developed freely? It is for this reason. The plant-leaf contains within it an etheric body adapted to the whole cosmic ether, which now comes to the aid of the egg of the gall-wasp. By itself, the egg is helpless. Thus the gall-wasp deposits it in a portion of the plant, which already contains an etheric body related to the whole system of the cosmic ether. The gall-wasp comes to the oak in order to bring about a complete breaking down of its albumen, so that the world periphery may be able to work *via* the oak-leaf, *via* the oak. The egg of the gall-wasp alone would be doomed to destruction, for it cannot be broken down, it is held together far too strongly.

Here indeed, we gain an insight into the strange workings of Nature, a working present in other places also. Assume for example, that the animal is not only unable to provide a germ substanceable to expose itself to the cosmic ether, but is also not even able to transform any substances within it into inner means of nourishment, that is, to use them for its own inner nourishment. The example of the bees lies near at hand. The bee cannot eat anything and everything; it can only eat what the plant has already prepared for it; and here is the strangest fact of all. The bee goes to the plant, seeks out the nectar, absorbs it, assimilates it within, and then builds up the wonderful cell structure of the honey-comb which we so greatly admire. Here we can observe two of the strangest and most wonderful processes; the bee sitting on the flower and sucking in its juices, and then having returned to the hive, building up from within itself, in connection with the other worker-bees, the cells of wax that they may fill them with honey.

What is actually taking place? You must carefully observe the shape of these cells. They are similar in form to something else we find in Nature, though here the hollowed space is filled up; they are formed like quartz crystals, like the crystals of silicic acid. If you go into the mountains and examine the quartz crystals you will find that you can draw them in the same form, but the cells the bees make are of wax, and the quartz crystals are of silicic acid.

When we follow this up further, we find that long ages ago, at a certain definite point in the evolution of the earth, these quartz crystals were first formed in the mountains. They were formed under the prevailing etheric and astral forces, with the aid of silicic acid. There you have the forces that come from the circumference, working as etheric and astral forces, and forming the quartz crystals in the silicious substance. Everywhere in the mountains you can find these crystals with their wonderful hexagonal forms. What you find in the solid crystals, you find again as hollow forms, as hollowed spaces, in the waxen cells in the bee-hive.

The bee takes up from the flower that which once upon a time brought the quartz crystal into being. The bee takes it from the flower, and from the substance of her own body makes an image of the quartz crystal. A process takes place between bee and flower that is similar to what took place in past ages in the Cosmos. I tell you these things that you may understand how necessary it is not merely to be aware of the presence of carbon, nitrogen, hydrogen and oxygen, of which all analysis is pitiably abstract, but to take into account the marvellous formative processes, the intimate inner conditions that prevail in Nature and her processes.

A Question and an Answer.

1. At the conclusion of one of the foregoing lectures, (December 10, 1923) a question was asked about the disease of "foulbrood." Dr. Steiner replied that as he had not yet studied this disease he could not make a definite statement. It might possibly be the result of a deficiency in the balance of the uric acid in the Queen bee. He said further : "The bee has also uric acid in its organism, and the cause of the disease will be found to be a wrong relationship in the uric acid."

2. In answer to a question as to the development of the bees from wasps, referred to in the same lecture, Dr. Steiner said : "This development occurred during the ancient Atlantean civilisation, when the individual animal forms were not so firmly established as today, when there were no such clearly defined boundaries between the different species. Today, such a thing would no longer be possible."

DIAGRAMS.

The coloured drawings by Dr. Rudolf Steiner have kindly been redrawn by Fraeulein E. Riese, but could be reproduced, unfortunately, only in black. The original colours are indicated.

TRANSLATIONS OF GERMAN WORDS USED IN THE DIAGRAMS
(IN ALPHABETICAL ORDER).

Figure 11. The down-streaming lines in the original copy are violet.

Figure 18. (a) Formic acid as the basis for soul and spirit.
(b) Formic acid as the basis for Earth-soul and Earth-spirit.

German	English	German	English
Aetherleib	ETHERIC BODY	Koenigin	QUEEN
Ameisensaeure	FORMIC ACID	Kohlensaeure	CARBONIC ACID
Arbeiterin	WORKER BEE	Leib	BODY
Astralleib	ASTRAL BODY	Menschl. Gewebe	HUMAN TISSUE
Biene	BEE	Milch	MILK
Blumensaft	FLOWER SAP	Mineralisch	MINERAL
Blut	BLOOD	Nerv	NERVE
Drohne	DRONE	Organisation	ORGANISATION
Gelb	YELLOW	Pflanzlich	PLANT
Gewebe	TISSUE	Phys. Leib	PHYSICAL BODY
Glyzerin	GLYCERINE	Quarz	QUARTZ
Gruenlich	GREENISH	Rot	READ
Haertere Zellen	HARDER CELLS	Tierisch	ANIMAL
Hohl	HOLLOW	Tiersaft	ANIMAL FLUIDS
Honig	HONEY	Violett	VIOLET
Ich	ORGANISATION, EGO-ORGANISATION	Weiss	WHITE
Insekten	INSECTS	Wespe	WASP
Kieselsaeure	SILICIC ACID	Zelle	CELL
Kleesaeure	OXALIC ACID		

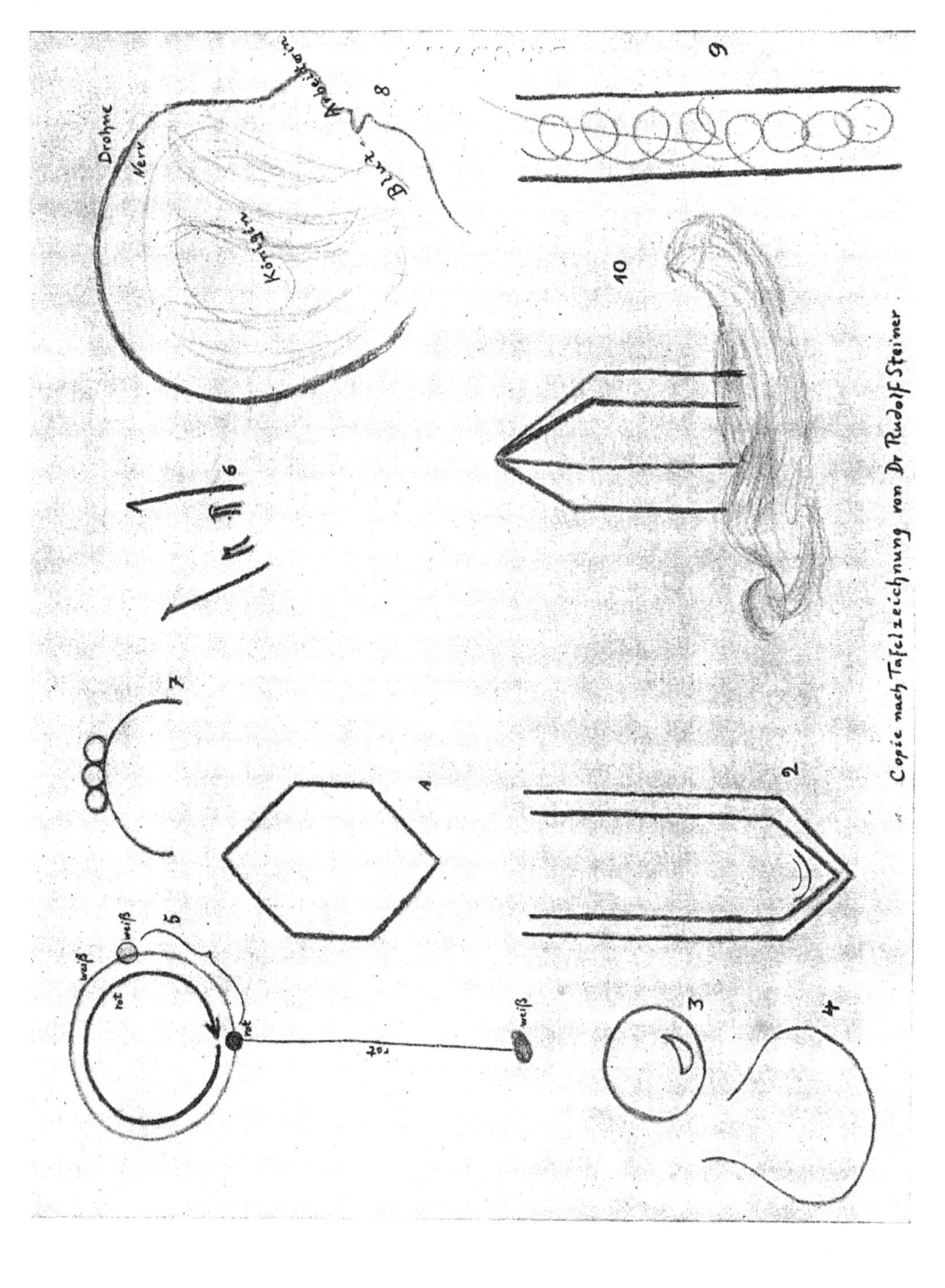

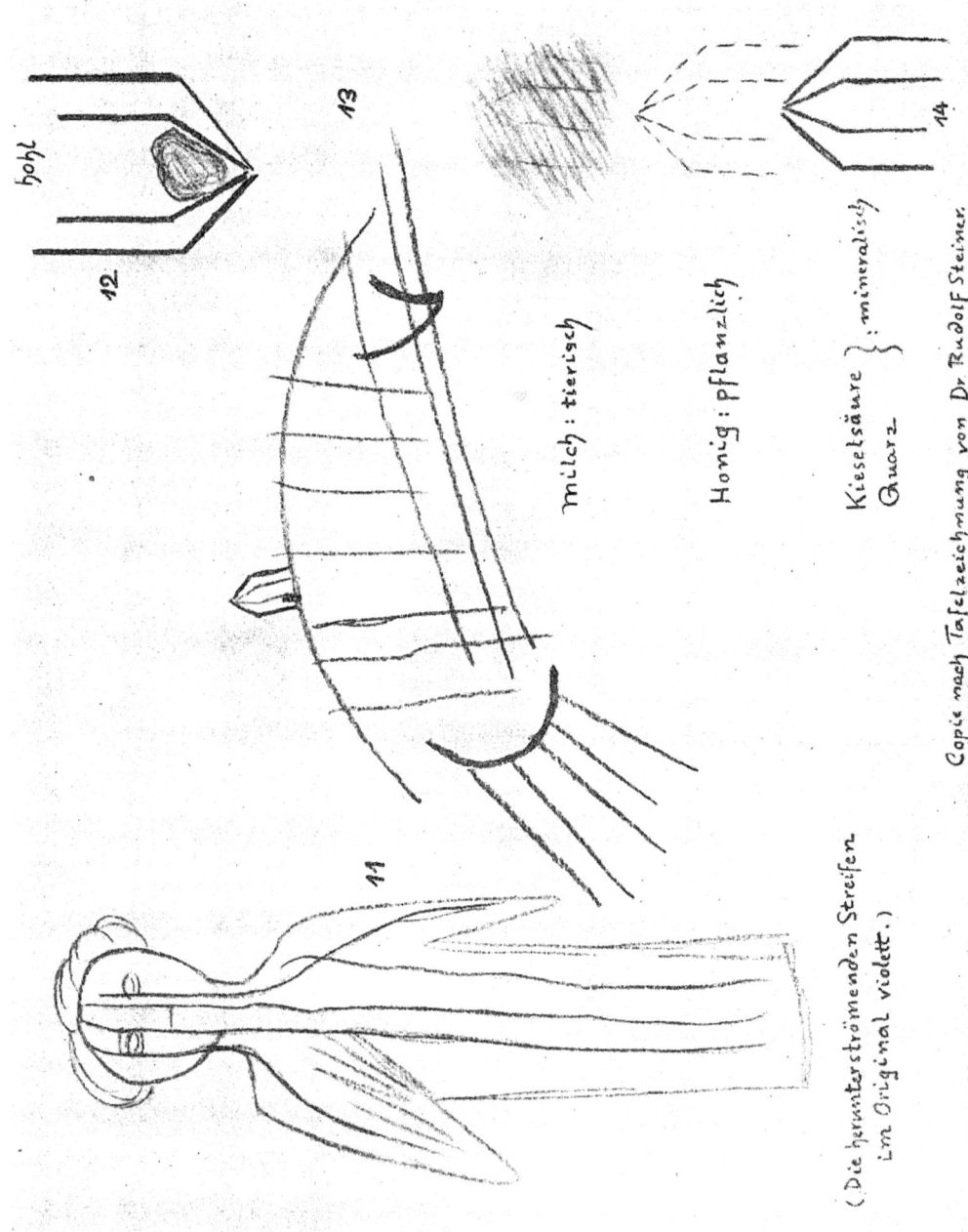

Biene: Blumensaft
Wespe: Blumensaft, Tiersaft: härtere Zellen
Ameise: Tiersaft: keine Zellen

1. Phys. Leib
2. Ätherleib
3. Astralleib
4. Ich-Organisation

Zeichnung 15.

Copie nach farbiger Tafelzeichnung von Dr. Rudolf Steiner

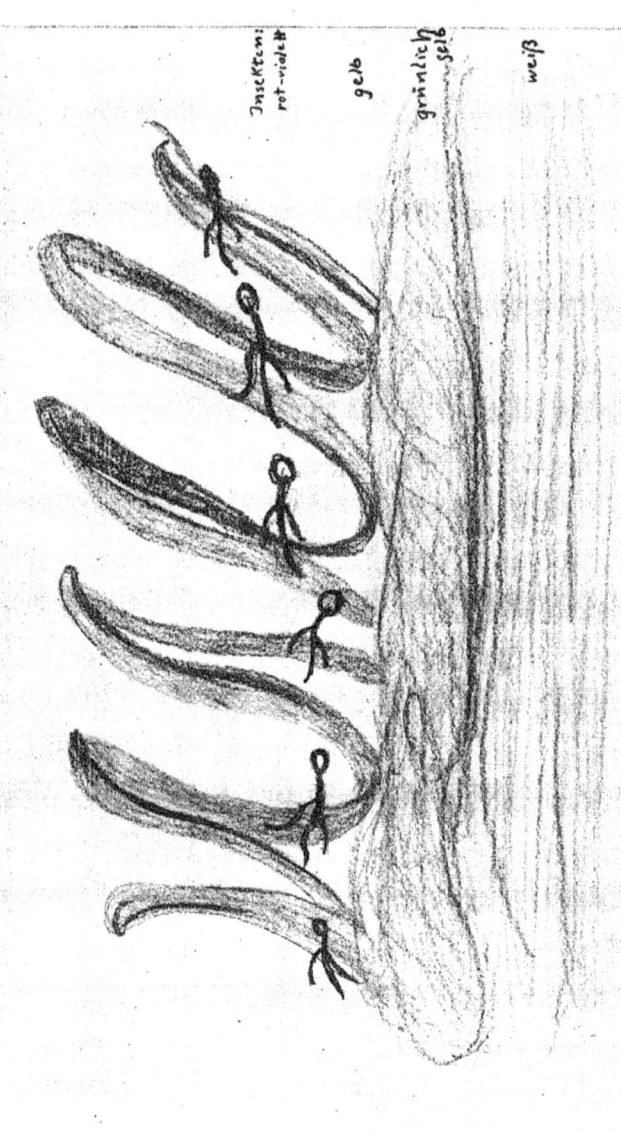

Insekten: rot-violett
gelb
grünlich gelb
weiß

Ameisensäure als Grundlage für Erdseele und Erdgeist.

Copie nach farbiger Tafelzeichnung von Dr. Rudolf Steiner.

Ameisensäure als Grundlage für Seele und Geist.

gelb u. weiß.

Zeichnung 18

16

17

Menschl. Gewebe.

Ameisensäure

Kohlensäure

Copie nach farbiger Tafelzeichnung von Dr. R. Steiner